CALMAN
AT THE
MOVIES

C000120615

Mel Calman

THE BODLEY HEAD
LONDON

First published 1990
© Mel Calman 1990
The Bodley Head Ltd, 20 Vauxhall Bridge Road, London SW1V 2SA

A CIP catalogue record for this book
is available from the British Library

ISBN 0-370-31391-7

Photoset by Rowland Phototypesetting Ltd, Bury St Edmunds, Suffolk
Printed in Great Britain by Butler and Tanner Ltd, Frome and London

Contents

Acknowledgments   vii
Introduction   1

Rod Steiger   7
Sir Alec Guinness   10
Lindsay Anderson   12
Robert Altman   15
Bob Ringwood   16
Jack Klaff   18
Allan Nicholls   20
Frederic Raphael   22
Verity Lambert   26
David Puttnam   28
Susannah York   31
Maurice Hatton   33
Ruth Goetz   36
Karel Reisz   38
Barry Norman   41
Ronald Harwood   44
Steve Abbott   48
Betsy Blair   50
Terence Stamp   53
Stephen Frears   56
Catherine Wyler   60
Richard Griffiths   63
Kitty Carlisle Hart   65
John Guare   68

Peter Yates   70
Jeremy Thomas   72
John Schlesinger   74
John Mortimer   77
Dick Clement & Ian La Frenais   82
Anne Coates   85
Mary-Anne Page   88
Tony Walton   90
Jonathan Lynn   94
Percy Adlon   97
Leah Adler   100
Roddy McDowall   103
Carrie Fisher   107
Billy Wilder   112
Saul Bass   113
Vincent Price & Coral Browne   116
Fiona Lewis   118
S. J. Perelman   121

Acknowledgments

I could never have written this book without the generous co-operation of all the people who found the time to talk to me. Some were friends, some were friends of friends and some were total strangers. I am indebted to all of them. I am also grateful to Otto Plashkes for his suggestions and introductions. My thanks to various helping hands: Gabrielle Kelly, Ian Moody, Claire Calman, Arnold Schwartzman and Deborah Moggach, who also listened very patiently to my doubts and insecurities. And thanks to Jane Fraser, Stephen Frears and Cathy Wyler for foolishly allowing me to stray on to their sets during production. And of course, Mike Shaw, of Curtis Brown, who thought it was a good idea in the first place and found a publisher.

And finally, I want to thank my pencil for...

Look - there's lovely Franklin Pangborn and.. quick.. that's Una Merkel - you know, the one you always confuse with Zasu Pitts. She was in that Stroheim movie (No. NOT Merkel - PITTS).. Isn't that Charlie Ruggles..he's the one you thought was Charles Laughton.. Remember they were in that movie we saw last Christmas - where Edward Arnold or do I mean Eugene Pallette?

Anyway...

A CLASSIC MOVIE

Introduction

My first visit to the cinema was very special. I was five years old. We lived in North London, and my parents took me to the Finsbury Park Astoria. This was one of those vast dream palaces that were built in the thirties to make filmgoers feel they lived exciting glamorous lives – escape hatches from the drab reality outside. The Astoria pretended to be a Moorish palace; with fountains, mosaic tiles, balconies and even a cascade of stars twinkling in a make-believe sky inside the auditorium. Tony Walton told me he used the Astoria to represent a luxury Turkish hotel in *Murder on the Orient Express* – so that gives you some idea of its opulence.

It was the cinema's birthday that week and there was a live stage show before the movie and a small piece of birthday cake for every child. I think it was the cake that clinched my love affair with the cinema.

As a schoolboy evacuated to Cambridge during the war I went as often as I could afford to go. In those days, there was a change of programme on Sundays, so you could snatch an extra helping of escapism on that dull day. Cambridge seemed to be always closed on Sundays – apart from the cinema and the Lyons tea-shop.

My older sister, Lydia, was a film reviewer for the *Cambridge Daily News*, and I often went with her to the Rex Cinema. I saw a great deal of tosh – Abbott and Costello, Nelson Eddy, Esther Williams – stuff that now appears very late at night on TV.

But it wasn't only junk food; there was some high-class

fibre as well. The Cosmo Cinema (now the Arts Cinema) showed foreign films and I fell in love with French fatalism. Arletty smiled at me and I was lost, without in any way giving up my existing deep passion for Rita Hayworth. *Un Carnet du Bal*, *Le Jour Se Lève*, *Les Enfants du Paradis* – the titles still have the power to make me feel like a teenager again, sitting in the dark wishing I were sophisticated and French. (And taller and less spotty, while God was listening.)

I had fantasies of becoming a film director when I grew up. Or at least a cinema manager who got to see the films for nothing. I read *Picturegoer* every week, relishing the brown and orange duotone photos of the stars. I also read serious books about the cinema. I was a curious mixture of film fan and cineaste -- if I had known the word. I self-consciously kept a notebook, where I wrote down the names of the directors of the films I saw, together with brief comments on the films themselves. If Fate had not stepped in, I might have become a film critic . . .

But I returned to London when I was eighteen and went to art school instead. I joined the British Film Institute and religiously went to all the archive classics every Friday at the Institute Française, South Kensington. This was in the early fifties, before they had built the National Film Theatre. *The Battleship Potemkin* joined 'The Good Ship Lollypop' inside my head. There must be a terrible clutter of styles and tastes in there.

Over the years I have continued going to the movies. I don't enjoy the large cupboards that have replaced the Astorias, but the love affair still burns. There is nothing to beat those opening moments in the dark, when the title appears and I settle down in my seat to watch someone else's dreams.

I first had the notion of doing this book when I was in Cannes during the Film Festival. I was sitting on the terrace of the Carlton Hotel, listening to two Americans lying to each other about their grosses, while crumbling croissants all over their Gucci sweaters. Suddenly I realized there was a whole

world I knew very little about. Movies were more than Rita
Hayworth or Jean Renoir. They were a madness and a
business as well as entertainment and art.

This book is an attempt to find out a little about the movie
world. I was curious to know why – and how – people got
into it. And what they liked and disliked about it. It is a taste
rather than a complete meal. But then I have always had a
weakness for snacks.

Ices, soft drinks, nostalgia, memories, seats at 1/9 pence..

Welcome to Cannes
NON!
Dont JUMP! Channel 4 may buy it...
This is not the time to decide you're bored with movies...
Easy to make 5 million in Germany alone
Fred has 4 and JAPAN has 150%.
200 E minin
Was that Lenn
World-

SEX, LIES & P.R.

...l interest you in a little co-production?

cliches & present a LEGENDARY

What a way to earn a living

TV

I hope it's not another SERBO-CROAT film with FRENCH subtitles...

...two omelettes, a Bottle of Evian and it cost £100. Who does Sean Connery think he is? on Tuesdays, Weds, THURS, FRI & SATURDAYS... y or Barry NORMAN? The bottom line is that FRED Hates it!...

If the worst comes to the worst - we can always INTERVIEW each other...

Cannes Film Festival...

Rod Steiger

Actor: 'On the Waterfront', 'The Pawnbroker', 'Doctor Zhivago', 'In the Heat of the Night', 'No Way to Treat a Lady', 'W. C. Fields and Me' and many others

I'm lucky to be in this business. If I wasn't I'd probably be a nasty drunk who got thrown out of pubs on Saturday nights. I didn't have much education – just one year at high school – I got an education from being in films. I drove an ice-truck at fourteen years of age, worked in a leather factory at sixteen and then I went into the Navy for five years. When I came out I went into the civil service. In the office on Thursdays all the pretty girls disappeared. We couldn't figure out why. Then we found out they were in this civil service theatre group, so all the boys went there to try to get lucky with the girls. We didn't know what we were doing, we didn't *care* what we were doing, we were just after the girls. After two plays the woman in charge said I should take it serious. I said 'You're joking.' Actors to me were golden people.

I came from a very poor family – you got 25 cents if you put out the garbage and did the dishes – but she reminded me I had the G I Bill of Rights, which gave you support, and I figured acting would be better than working in the civil service. After about two months I became a fanatic about it.

The thing that started me was the original *Marty*, which I did for television. That got me into movies. Kazan was looking for somebody to play Marlon Brando's brother in *On the Waterfront*. After that I did nine pictures in a row.

Kazan was one of the best directors for an actor because he was a very good actor himself. He doesn't deal in results. He doesn't say 'Get angry here.' He gives you a reason to get angry. If a director doesn't know people he's not going to get anywhere. Kazan could pick out the things that upset you just by talking to you.

I'm glad I portrayed W. C. Fields in the biographic movie because he was brilliant. He was also one of the loneliest, most miserable men I ever met, I mean *played*. He was the world's greatest juggler and you certainly can't be drunk and do that. When he started dropping things he'd say a line and people would begin to laugh. If he didn't like you he would insist on teaching you how to juggle a knife and fork and you would be slicing yourself to death. 'You can do it once more, my darling.' He was terrible.

We now have a new disease: the kids who come through from television. They go into a movie and last about five years because they never did anything to develop themselves. Then the series is over and they end up on dope and alcohol.

How do I cope with setbacks? Oh, I just go into four-year depressions. I didn't work for four years at one stage because of depression. If it hadn't been for my wife I probably would have finished up killing myself. She got me through it.

If you try to make your life out of this kind of stuff, like Cannes, you're gonna be a miserable person. The danger is that you start to believe in all this. I'm lucky because I came from a poor family and I never trust anything now. If it all disappeared tomorrow I'd say, 'That's the way it is. I knew this was gonna happen.'

I would have liked to have been a good poet. I've got about 400 poems. God knows what they're like. I'd like to have one published that the general public remembered. I'd rather have people going round quoting a line from one of my poems than have them remember any of my films.

Sir Alec Guinness

Actor

It was never my ambition to be in films. The first time I ever appeared, purely as a walk-on, was in the summer of 1933, when I was a drama student. I used to walk barefoot in the summer to save shoe-leather and I was strolling through Hyde Park when I got into conversation with some young man who turned out to be an assistant film director – I didn't know what the heck that was – and he said, why don't you come down to the studio and I'll get you a day's work. That meant a pound, which was terrific.

The film was *Evensong*, directed by Victor Saville, with Evelyn Laye. I went down at some unearthly hour in the morning to Ealing Studios. I was then dressed as a 1914 Tommy; with a great crowd of others we were herded around like cattle and shouted at. The whole thing was so remote from any life I wanted. I collected my pound and swore I would never go into a studio again, or at least until I knew what I was doing. And I didn't until 1945 with *Great Expectations*.

It's awfully difficult to know how to occupy one's time while waiting around on films. I wrote the screenplay for *The Horse's Mouth* when working on a film which was very boring. I also took to making flies for fly fishing. Of course the moment one got set up on a table in a corner, with a feather and a bit of silk in your mouth, they would shout, 'Ready'.

I have been in some films with hardly any make-up at all. I used to beg directors to make my first shot in the film – my first impact – a long shot because I felt I could convey more of the character through my whole body rather than just my face. I still like that.

I don't think I'm a very good film actor, technically. I can hit my marks wonderfully. I used to be very stiff and self-conscious, and such technical skill (which is minimal) which I have, I suppose I learned from David Lean and those few early films I did with him.

I like to get away from myself as an actor. Or I used to, but now that I'm seventy-five, I don't.

Lindsay Anderson

Director: 'This Sporting Life', 'If', 'O Lucky Man',
'The Whales of August' and others

At Oxford I was very keen on films, but only as a fan. I didn't
even know what a director *was*. In those days nobody knew
anything; nowadays everybody knows *everything*. There was
one book about movies, a Penguin book by Roger Manvell
called *Film* – oh yes, and Paul Rotha: *The Film Till Now*.

I met a lady who was married to the managing director of
a firm in Yorkshire that made conveyor belts – 'The World
Pioneers of Underground Belt Conveying'. She was a film fan.
When I came down from Oxford this lady turned up out of
the blue and said, 'My husband's company wants you to make
a film celebrating the fiftieth anniversary of the firm.' I said,
'You're crazy. I don't know anything about making a film.
I've never touched any pieces of film equipment in my life.'
She said, 'You've got to start somewhere.' So I started making
industrial films, and I also edited a magazine called *Sequence*
with Gavin Lambert.

In 1956 I made this film about a funfair in Margate, called
Oh, Dreamland. Lorenza Mazetta had made a film called
Together, and Karel Reisz and Tony Richardson had made
their film *Momma Don't Allow*. We thought: What are we
going to do with these films? I had the idea of calling it 'Free
Cinema', because you've got to give journalists something to
write about. So we called it a movement. That way we got
much more publicity. The films were shown at the NFT; it
was very exciting. This is all pre-history now. I always tell
young film-makers: Get together and call yourself a movement. But they're all too egotistical.

1956 was a fantastic year – the opening of the Royal Court, Hungary, Suez. I became Associate Director at the Court and didn't make any films for two or three years. Then I read a book called *This Sporting Life* and had a feeling it would make a good film. I suggested it to Tony Richardson. At that time of cohesive, friendly activity – the Court, Free Cinema – we all knew each other. Tony had started *Look Back in Anger* as a film, and *The Entertainer*. He had also made a great contribution as a producer, enabling Karel Reisz to make *Saturday Night and Sunday Morning* – of any film, this was the one that most changed things.

One of my problems is that the films I've made have been mixtures of romance and satire, very ambiguous; and people don't really expect to think, when they go to the cinema – they don't want to think. That goes for critics, too. If you confront them with this mixture they'll call you confused.

What's wrong with films now? An increased emphasis on effect – on the look of the film. Show-off stuff. Critics refer to 'stunning camerawork'; but the ability to tell a story and create empathy with your characters, that has been largely lost. There's a great deficiency, now, in seriousness. Take a director like John Ford: he was a poet, and also a moralist. That's what gave his work substance. It's the climate nowadays, it's part of the flight from emotion, the flight from feeling. It's the era of Tom Stoppard and Martin Amis – absolutely cold. If you want the quintessential artistic flavour today, watch Martin Amis being interviewed by Melvyn Bragg on the 'South Bank Show' and you've got it in a nutshell.

I'd like to have made more films. It must have been wonderful to have been an American director in the thirties, to have been Ford and made film after film – quite apart from the fact that he was a genius. But I know I'm what's called 'difficult' – I've been told so often enough. I'm acerbic and I speak my mind. I remember at school, Cheltenham College, I was walking along the quad with my form-master, a nice chap. There had been some sort of row and he said, 'You know,

I'd like to be 'persona non grata' when I grow up, sir..

Anderson, if you go on like this you'll be *persona non grata* with an awful lot of people.' And I said, 'Yes sir, I expect you're right but I'm afraid it's too late to change.'

I'm also very subjective, so I've only made films I'm very subjectively involved in. That means people don't offer me other kinds of films because I seem to have put myself into a category. Last year, when I went to Toronto to film a mini-series for American TV, it was one of the very first things I've been sent out of the blue like that, as if I were a professional film-maker! I'm generally regarded as some sort of freak. When I was sent the script, I liked it. So I thought: Well, I'll have a go, I'll see if I'm the same as everybody else; everybody else does these things and I don't because I'm supposed to have such 'integrity', which is very boring. It bores everyone else, including myself.

It had to be shot very quickly – three and a half hours in 35 days – and when I said to the Canadian assistant, 'How can we do it?' he replied, 'With grace and humour.' After we finished it I thought: They can't say I'm not a proper professional now. I haven't noticed them saying I *am* a proper professional film-maker, but never mind.

Robert Altman

Director: 'Mash', 'Nashville', 'A Wedding' and many others

I came from Kansas City – a hick town in the Midwest. Everybody went to the movies – the way Spanish kids go to the bullfights. We'd go on binges – from movie to movie – maybe three in a day.

I was a pilot in the Second World War and I wrote short stories. A friend of mine was working as a director for a company making industrial films and he said, come on down. So I went and they were looking for directors. I got a job as a director. I lied a lot. I didn't know very much but I knew enough to lie. I was there for six years.

You did everything: writing . . . casting . . . shooting . . . editing . . . the sound. That's how I got into it. It's that theatrical thing of working four days and nights to get it opened and then the whole thing is swept away. You get to combine the three acts of a lifetime into this tight space. It affords you the chance to live lots of different lives. Complete – with a beginning, a middle and an end. You get thrown into new people, new enthusiasms.

It's like making children: I look at the films I've done and I like them all. You tend to love your least successful children best.

What I do is very collaborative – I don't have to finish everything myself. I start one pot boiling and then go and stir the next pot and keep them all bubbling. It's like *pommes frites* – the ones that come to the top and pop are finished.

Bob Ringwood

Costume designer: 'Empire of the Sun', 'Batman',
'Chicago Joe and the Showgirl'

Directors don't know anything about costume design. It's something they don't understand. I met Spielberg for twenty minutes when I was designing for *Empire of the Sun* . . . 10,000 costumes. It staggers me how un-visual film directors are. Their job is an intellectual one rather than a visual one.

Film-making attracts two types of personality. Half the business is run by thugs or gangsters – oiks that don't lift their noses out of the trough. On the other side you've got people who often aren't conscious of money. They just love the film world. I have to confess I went into it for the money. I was doing the same job in the theatre and starving to death. I figured I might as well do the same job in the cinema and earn six times as much. I do love it though.

I've only done one film where I thought the script wasn't really up to it. It was about orphans in the future running away from the authorities on roller-skates in the desert. After reading the script my first question was, how do you roller-skate in the sand?

I enjoyed *Batman* but with a bit more money I think we could have got a stronger look in the crowd. Jack Nicholson was wonderful because he really is that character. He lives it. He's an absolute object lesson in how to behave as an actor. He's funny, charming and witty. One minute he'd be in his dressing-room reading some obscure Russian novel, the next minute chasing some floosie on the set.

Designing for the theatre is much coarser. In the cinema the camera's going to be one inch from the actor's nose, so the whole thing has to be much more refined. I always say you don't smell the screen. You might be filming in a sewer, but on the screen it looks like a rose garden.

You get complaints all the time of course. The actors playing the smaller parts feel neglected because the director doesn't speak to them. So they whinge endlessly. For them the next best thing is to get to the dressing-room and complain about the shoes or whatever. They feel insecure and want to be loved. We're the people who have to do it.

You can go through hell with some of the more neurotic actresses. You get huge dramas over the shape of an earring or whatever. I usually give them a gin and that generally keeps them happy. Some people – usually Americans – are just out for trouble. They think that's how Bette Davis would have behaved.

In my experience all the big stars I've worked with haven't been like that. Failed actors are the worst, alcoholic ones in particular. I've actually given people tumblers of whisky just to get them on the set. I've worked with several 'reformed' alcoholics who hide liquor everywhere. You keep finding strange bottles – usually medicine bottles – hidden away. It's terribly funny, but it's also terribly sad. On the whole most of them are sweet enough.

You might be the most wonderful designer in the world but if you don't get the person on-stage, in the right clothes and feeling good, you haven't done your job. It's a bit like running a country and not going into debt. I always try and stay on budget. It can cost a lot of money if you hold up a shoot – all that expensive equipment and all those people on massive salaries standing around. If you forget to bring the shoes, you're fired.

I was hoping to get Best Supporting Role...

Jack Klaff

Actor: 'King David' etc.

My agent phoned me up with the leading part in this novel. There were two characters: one very beautiful blond man and one really weird guy with one eye and a moustache. As I'm dark and not very blond, I assumed they'd want me for the weird guy. So I grew a moustache and put one contact lens in. But when I walked in, he said he wanted me for the blond character.

There's this guy who imitates chimpanzees. They were doing a film with real chimps and the director told him to go in and help the real chimpanzees to be more chimp-like for the movie.

On *King David* we were filming in Italy because it was supposed to be Jerusalem. One day it hailed and we figured there was no way we'd film so we started to do some very silly things. The driver had stolen a case of wine from the catering tent and we got drunk. Unfortunately, the hail stopped and we had to work. They wheeled us up to go and watch Goliath being killed. You've got to be hot and sober watching this really important moment and we were shivering because it was so cold.

They couldn't afford the extras. If you're going to make a biblical epic, you've got to have lots of extras. They thought they'd have Italians, you see, and they thought these guys would be cheap. They wanted 10,000 people but had to make do with only 2,000.

It's the one time in my life I was able to tell someone I was taking chariot-riding lessons. A friend asked me to join him

for lunch, and I said, rather grandly, 'Sorry, I can't come –
I'm having chariot lessons.' And I went to Shepherd's Bush
and had these lessons in how to drive a chariot. That's movies.

Allan Nicholls

Assistant director: 'Nashville', 'A Wedding'

Studio heads have this idea that film-making is about making money. Nothing else. It's not about making films any more. That's the scariest thing for me. I got into it because it was an art form. Now it's a money thing and the people that give you the money tell you what to do. It's like standing over Van Gogh and saying, 'The yellow is wrong. I think you should be using a beige there.'

There were enough characters in *A Wedding* for them to distribute the writing between three different writers. We were in this mansion outside Chicago. We'd sit in this room upstairs and hack away, trading off each other. It was a great collaboration because you'd all be writing your individual scene for those particular characters you chose, but then you'd pass it on to John or Pat and then we'd deliver it to Bob Altman. He can always make a line just a little bit better.

The union rules make film-making so costly. They've put crews in a position where some of these guys can be making 150 dollars an hour overtime. At some point they can get into a situation where they're on double-double time – what they call 'platinum time'.

They now have this rule where a truck over 20 foot long requires two drivers – a driver and a helper. They make 37 dollars an hour each to drive a truck. Rules like these have gotten studios into situations where they can't take risks.

If directors have anything in common, it's ego. As much as you want to say there's no one star, usually the director wants to be the focus. It's gotten to the level now where stars can dictate who they want as a director. I'm at the stage now where I'm ready to direct and if that situation came about for me I think it would be really discouraging. It has crossed my mind that maybe I'm not hungry enough ego-wise.

Frederic Raphael

Writer: 'Darling', 'Two for the Road', 'Nothing But the Best', 'A Severed Head', 'Daisy Miller', 'Far from the Madding Crowd' and others

My first involvement with Hollywood was Hollywood London, because in the middish sixties a lot of Hollywood people came here. The first person I met was Stanley Donen. He'd seen a movie I'd written, *Nothing But the Best*, and he'd liked it. So he called me and said 'Let's do something.'

He had a great reputation going back to *On the Town* and *Singin' in the Rain*. Being approached by a legendary movie-maker – not a *film-maker*, not a kind of cinema buff, but a movie-maker – made one think, Hey! One: Hey, this is the real big movies. Two: Hey, perhaps I'm going to be rich; which is one of those great unadmitted elements in people's considerations. No one ever admits to being at all interested in money but I notice that most people are unreluctant to accept it when it's forced on them. Funnily enough, again a thing rarely admitted by so-called artists, it doesn't half prime the imagination.

So I thought up the movie, which turned out to be *Two for the Road* with Albert Finney and Audrey Hepburn. It was of course well pissed on by all the Brits who knew how dreadfully I'd sold out, and it's now taught in all the film schools, doubtless on account of Audrey Hepburn, Albert Finney and Stanley Donen and not on account of me, but I wouldn't like to be told that by anybody.

Then I won the Oscar for *Darling* which, as is often said, is both an accolade and a sentence of death. This is because it tends to be the crowning, if not the entombing element in people's careers, rather than the moment of great opportunity.

And funnily enough – not very funny to me but a source of great comfort to moralists – I've never actually had a Hollywood movie made since. I've made other films, and TV of course, and I'm writing a movie at the moment for somebody in California. But I've not saddled another Hollywood winner – not even a runner.

I've written other scripts, but they just don't get made. One of the reasons is the latest appalling confession by an executive out there (we live in the age of executives). He said, 'Listen, what we're looking for in the movie business right now is "no-brainers".' It's a wonderful phrase and an appalling prospect. Nowadays they won't read your script. They won't even read the 'coverage' on your script, which is the report on it by recent graduates of creative writing and film schools who know much more than you do even though you've been writing for forty years. What they do is read the title. '*Mom, I Shrank the Kids!* Let's do it!' 'Don't you want to see the script?' 'No, let's do it! Great! Great!' If you can't say it in a sentence, get out of the office. It's always been a bit like that. But like everything that's been a *bit* like that, on the whole it's getting worse.

If a studio says it's a great script you have absolutely no notion that they're going to do it – indeed, that's usually the apologetic rather than the encouraging form. The good news is, 'X has a call, but he's doing your script.' Which means that if they need you again they'll call you, otherwise the director will go about the usual directorial business of ruining the jokes, rearranging the plot and taking the credit. The main talent of directors – apart from the very few who are very good – can be simply encapsulated as 'getting the job'. The only time you ever meet a director who is courteous, interested, and seeking in every way to impress you, is when he fears that you may have some influence on whether or not he gets the job. Once he's got it, the talent which he admired before curiously becomes his, not yours.

Why on earth does one go on doing it? Because if you write

dialogue it's fun to have it performed, and it's not particularly fun to have it performed by the Bognor Regis Dramatic Society. If you're going to be a player you want to play on the Centre Court or at the top table. The fun of it is the endless, fugitive and evasive prospect of doing something wonderful on a global scale. Hollywood is a gamble. The table is there, the wheel spins and – hey! – if you hit, you hit. Meanwhile they pay you quite a lot of money for losing.

One of the dangers of 'pitching' is the ease with which you can talk yourself into something even as you're refusing to do it. Some time ago, two producer friends of mine, David Brown and Richard Zanuck, had bought a book about Sir Walter Raleigh. It was called, I think, *The Day of the Fox*. One of the things they do out there is get 'auction-happy', which means buying books they haven't read simply because other people want them. This one was showy, mock-Elizabethan stuff written by an American academic – in other words it was totally unperformable and couldn't be turned into a screenplay. I told my two friends this, over lunch. At which point (typical response) they said, 'That's why we thought of you!'

Cut to: there I am, doing it. I can't use any of the book, but I find Sir Walter Raleigh interesting and I write, I think, a very nice screenplay.

I sent it off to them. I got back an immediate, three-page telegram saying, 'This is great. It's going to be the greatest screenplay that ever came through the studio; we're going to get the greatest director in the world, etc. etc. Meanwhile, love and kisses.'

So, nothing happens. Nothing. Then, six months later, the same studio rings up and says, 'Freddie, we'd love you to do a screenplay about a thing that happened in France. We have a director in mind. Could you come out and talk about it?' So I thought, Why not? A trip to California; two first-class fares. Worse things have happened to people. Like having to depend for one's future on Auberon Waugh.

So I flew out to California to talk about this entirely new French project. All goes very well, lovely to see you again, and then I said, 'Do you remember *The Day of the Fox*? What happened to that?' And they said, 'Wow, what a screenplay! That was probably the greatest screenplay that has ever been through this studio!' I said, 'Yes, that's terrific, I know you said that, I'm so glad you think so. What's happened to it?' And they said, 'Freddie, listen. We admired the hell out of that script, but who the fuck is Sir Walter Raleigh?'

In the thirties or forties, when film was supposedly in its golden age (actually a lot of those films were dreadful beyond belief), there was a feeling that there was a uniform culture to which all Americans aspired. The rise of ethnicity has been a disaster for intelligent films. Though they like jokes, they don't like the smart wisecracks of *The Philadelphia Story* – that's not what the Hispanics and the blacks think they *ought* to be like, anymore.

The Jews, on the other hand, imagined that they could be *real* Americans and they therefore *invented* real Americans – who had never really existed. Hollywood created the idea of what a WASP was. Andy Hardy is Louis B. Mayer's idea of what he could never be.

Verity Lambert

Producer: 'A Cry in the Dark', 'Dr Who' (TV).
Director of Productions: EMI Euston Films

The beginning of my career was extremely mundane. I left school at sixteen and didn't have a clue what I wanted to do. I just knew I didn't want to be a secretary, but my mother insisted I have something to fall back on, so I did take a secretarial course.

I got a job at Granada. Commercial television was just beginning. I wasn't a very good secretary. I worked for a wonderful woman who was actually a director, but was somehow the press officer at Granada. It really was a case of the blind leading the blind.

I then became a production assistant before starting *Dr Who* in 1963 at the BBC. I was the first woman drama producer and also about twenty years younger than all the male producers. When people were introduced to me a look of horror flashed across their faces before they rearranged them into polite smiles.

Quite a few of them were rather cynical. They either tried to patronize me or hoped I'd fall flat on my face. But I found that being a woman can be a positive advantage. You can be a lot more outspoken. You can get away with saying things that men can't. You can be blunt. But there still aren't many women producers.

A Cry in the Dark was a wonderful experience, but the Golan brothers had a very middle-eastern attitude towards women and it was extremely difficult for them to treat me in any way like a human being. If you're working for megalomaniacs the fact that *you* got Meryl Streep soon turns into *they* got Meryl Streep and if you point out the fact that it isn't true, they don't like it. I think they found it 'unpalatable' when they realized I wouldn't be pushed around.

Of course there are a lot of gangsters in the movie business. In Hollywood if some of those people weren't running film studios they'd be running the Mafia. At least in the Mafia there's some kind of loyalty to the family.

David Puttnam

Producer: 'Chariots of Fire', 'Midnight Express', 'The Killing Fields' etc.

There were two absolutely fundamental moments that hooked me on making movies that I remember vividly. When I was seven the lady next-door took me to see *Pinocchio*. I'd never seen a film before. I even remember there was a short – *Steamboat Willy* – and I couldn't believe it. It knocked my socks off. Midway through, half of me stopped watching the film and started watching the people watching the film. What an amazing experience – all these people roaring with laughter. I remember thinking what a wonderful thing to do, to make people feel this way. And then I went to see *Bambi* about six months later. That was the first time I'd seen people cry. Then I saw *Snow White* and I was frightened. But for the first four or five years all I ever saw was animated films. I didn't even know there was such a thing as live action.

Then just before I left school I saw *Inherit the Wind* and that was the first time I realized the power of debate and ideas. What happened in that film was that my mind kept changing – similar to when I saw *Twelve Angry Men* the first time – and it made me realize what a crummy school I was at and what a rubbishy education I was getting because we didn't debate ideas. We were just stuck with facts.

When I left school my father got me a job as a messenger in an advertising agency. Then I went through a period of fanatically going to the movies, two or three times a week. I joined the NFT and started getting into heavy movies. At that time I was playing tennis quite seriously and right by the NFT there used to be two sunken tennis courts – where the walkway

now is on the South Bank – and my friend and I used to run from the office, book the court, play an hour's tennis and then go to the NFT.

I'll only ever move on if I become convinced in my own mind that the cinema has left me. By that I mean if the only films people are interested in seeing and the only films possible to finance are films that I don't want to be involved in, then I'll go. I'm not going to cling on. I'm lucky I can say that. I'd rather make documentaries about animals for survival, work for the BBC. What I'm not going to do, like many producers in their sixties and seventies, is cling on for that one more movie.

Probably the least creative eighteen months of my life was in Hollywood, at Columbia. There was no time to think, you were just reacting all the time. You can do nothing else all day but answer phones. We once logged all the callers – 135 by lunchtime. Most days there were between fifteen and seventeen meetings. We always had a breakfast meeting and always a dinner one at 8.30. It was the same at weekends. I got so tense I couldn't move my shoulders.

People in the American film industry know the chance of their producing anything wonderful is negligible.

The best bits I like about making films are the scriptwriting and the post-production. With scriptwriting the weather's always perfect! You've never got to worry about the weather when you're working on a script. It's sunny when you want it to be sunny, raining when you want it to rain, foggy when you want it foggy. Script is control. I love post-production. I love the cutting room and I love the mixing process. You haven't got to talk to the actors anymore. You haven't got to worry about the weather. The filming process itself is a nightmare.

I find directors tend to be less honest than producers. I think they frequently hide behind high intent when often what you're dealing with is low purpose. The job description is so damaging. I feel sorry for film directors in a way because the ethos and the culture of a film director – what a film director is – is so out of whack with what the job really is. I'm sure a lot of them have a tremendous problem not wearing jodhpurs. They're acting out a role.

You make 5,000 to 7,000 decisions when you're making a film. If you get 80 per cent of them right you've got a great film on your hands. It's all about percentages. I think so much of life is about percentages.

Susannah York

Actress: 'Tunes of Glory', 'The Greengage Summer', 'Tom Jones', 'A Man For All Seasons', 'The Killing of Sister George', 'Images' and others

I wanted to be an actress from the word go. I'd written plays from the age of seven, bagging the best parts for myself. I was nine when I got my first real laugh – at the village hall in Troon. I'd been cast as one of the ugly sisters in *Cinderella* and I suppose that experience taught me that the best parts aren't necessarily goodies.

At the beginning of my career I took films for granted. I thought they were for pretty people and the real acting was done on the stage.

There came a point when I'd done maybe four films and I became terror-struck. I thought I might lose my nerve and never be able to go on stage again, so I went back into the theatre.

I've always been amazed by actors who say there's a difference between the technique for film acting and the theatre. The essence of acting is the same. Immediacy seems to me to be the cardinal thing in acting. Very few people are really endowed with pure, natural technique. You have to work and work and work at it. It's a question of re-achieving spontaneity.

The pleasure of acting is being different people. The camera and the technicians are your audience when you're acting in the movies. There is a great pleasure in having a camera come into your eyes and knowing that what is there in your eyes, what is happening to you, will be picked up absolutely and transmitted.

That is more difficult on stage. The camera doesn't come

If we get any more intimate we'll have to propose marriage

into you; you go out to the audience. The camera doesn't lie. But the intimacy of the camera is wonderful. You have to be able to be vulnerable to it; to allow it to invade your being.

The quality I look for in a director is trust. All actors are insecure and if they feel a director doesn't trust them it upsets them. If they feel he does they can go over the top and do more. If you're not always testing the limits you fall short, but the director must have the authority to be able to stop you. You have always got to remember that he has chosen you.

Directors don't always have a visual sense *and* a love of words. Altman does. He has a brilliant aural sense; an ear for what happens in life when dialogues thread in and out.

People tend not to have very elastic minds in this business. It's often very difficult for them to make jumps. They lack imagination, especially the money men. Actors develop and grow and change. We are all amateur psychologists and we're in the business because of our fascination with the human race.

Maurice Hatton

Writer, director and independent film-maker: 'Praise Marx and Pass the Ammunition', 'Long Shot', 'American Roulette' and others

I was originally a photographer, working in journalism. At a certain stage I began to feel that the things I was covering would be more interesting on film. This was in the early sixties, when there wasn't an independent cinema. But I got together with two other people and we formed a company called Mithras, with the intention of making the kind of films we wanted, which were originally documentaries, and with a view to making a living out of it. This was considered quite bizarre. People didn't do that, then.

Our first film was a documentary about the Durham Miners' Gala. We went up there and I was given a 16mm Arriflex, which I'd never handled before. But from my photography I knew about exposure and focus. They said, 'Go off and shoot what you like.' Several people were filming at the same time.

So I responded to what was happening, and began to follow people – to move with them and move back with them. I figured that if I used a wide-angle lens, they would remain in focus and it would seem as if the movement was less obvious. Then I suddenly saw that the other people were standing around watching me, amazed. They said, 'You can't do that. You can't move with the camera.' And I said, 'Why not?' They said, 'You have to have it on a proper tripod.'

But when we came to see the rushes, my stuff was fantastic, because I'd hit on the essential thing – which was simultaneously being discovered by the New Wave in France – and this was that if you follow a moving object and you've got a wide-angle, the camera movement is not obvious.

Our first feature film was *Praise Marx and Pass the Ammunition* with John Thaw. It was made for practically nothing – the budget was tiny. Money determines the final look of a film. With money you can stay shooting longer, use more people, re-shoot a scene if it hasn't worked, and do more tracking shots, which are very time-consuming. Without money you have to construct self-enclosed scenes, and not use a lot of crowd or exterior scenes. Your material means determine a lot of aesthetic choices.

I suppose I've stayed an independent partly because of my temperament and partly because of the subject-matter I use. Besides, once you've established yourself as someone who writes, produces, directs and edits your own films, other producers are understandably reluctant to want to employ you on their projects.

The most difficult thing is that you can't practise and learn your craft unless you're in work. You can do ads, and TV, but this is limiting. At a certain point you have the technical skills, but your material is restricting. If you look at many TV dramas, they don't need any more elaborate or ambitious techniques. They don't require an individual voice. So I tend not to confuse the two. It's also hard for people like me, in England, who want to tackle moral content with a comic perspective. This lies uneasily on the English soul.

It's funny – everyone thinks they can direct a film. Not everybody thinks they can be a brain surgeon, but they think they can direct a film. They think you stand there and tell the camera to do that. Also, everybody has movies in their mind – they're part of our lives. The most illuminating experience, for anyone, is to say to them, 'Here's a video camera. Construct a scene.' The gap between what's in their head, and what comes on the screen, is devastating. It's a cliché, but still it's true: the more you know, the more you realize how little you know.

This is an INDEPENDENT film — which means you PAY me for being in it...

Ruth Goetz

Writer (with Augustus Goetz): 'The Heiress' and various screenplays, including 'Carrie'

I'd always gone to movies. I had a nursemaid, a French girl called Louisa, who took me every afternoon away for lunch. But what she would really do was to take the money my mother had given her for lunch and she would take me up Broadway – Broadway was then a parade of movie houses – and we would go in all afternoon and then we would go home. And I thank God for Louisa; because thanks to her I saw all the movies I had to know about. I was four. I was in a movie house *every* afternoon of my life for about a year and a half, before my mother found out. The lunch money bought the tickets . . . I was a little thinner but I was very entertained . . . (laughs). I saw *The Birth of a Nation*, which I would never have seen otherwise. I had watched a lot of stories being told. Certainly my education never helped. I adored Louisa.

I worked for Goldwyn as a story editor for about a year,

to read stuff and collect material. I was hired by George Oppenheimer . . . and then, when Goldwyn fired George I was immediately fired. Being employed in the movie business was always a matter of the kite and the tail. When the kite fell, the tail was immediately destroyed. If a director was fired, everyone he had brought in was fired.

When Paramount bought *The Heiress* in 1947, they asked us to write the screenplay. 'How much will they pay us?' I asked our agent, and she said, 'Two thousand dollars each a week.' I thought it was a lot of money then and it's still a lot of money.

At Paramount we had writers' rooms. We wrote and then Wyler would read it daily. Wyler was the producer of *The Heiress* as well as the director.

We walked over to the commissary every day for lunch. Cecil B. de Mille had a long table which stretched down one side. At about five minutes to one, he would walk in and he would have two secretaries, one on either side. He would dictate to both women. The writers would sit in successive rows . . . the top writers would be next to de Mille and then the lesser writers and finally, at the bottom, were the poor schmucks who actually wrote the stuff. He talked during lunch, and they took down every word – including the menu. They would type it all up . . . and it's still there somewhere in the Paramount archives.

Karel Reisz

Director: 'Saturday Night and Sunday Morning',
'Morgan: A Suitable Case for Treatment', 'Isadora',
'The Gambler', 'The French Lieutenant's Woman'

The most important thing about directing is to make people
think you know what you're doing. It's quite difficult sometimes because you turn up on location and there are the forty
lorries, or whatever, and the light isn't the way you'd hoped
for it and everybody says 'What are we going to do now,
guvnor?' and you haven't got an idea in your head. So the
first hour of every day's shooting is fairly agonizing.

However much you plan the stuff, if you don't lay yourself
open to what's happening *on that day* it turns out dead. I find
that if I plan a scene the night before and I think I know
where the camera's going to go and everything, it's always
wrong. I can't really start until I get the actors with their lines
trying it this way and trying it that way, then out of that you
somehow muddle through to a camera position. But the
Spielberg version of movie-making, or the Hitchcock version,

Everyone thinks I know what I'm doing
except ME!

knowing *exactly* what you want and then illustrating it, is simply a different world.

Directing is all about acting as far as I'm concerned. A lot of directors don't like actors, they don't *speak* to actors. A lot of what actors suffer is pure funk and it's part of a director's job to absorb that and not get thrown too much. I do like actors, though. I have a good time with actors. They're so brave. They show you their soul at 8.30 in the morning.

Editing is the best time. It's the only stage in a film when you're not working under the gun, because often the problem is not 'Are we doing it well?' but 'Are we going to get it *done*?'

The process of film-making either turns you on or it doesn't. If it does it's really addictive. I used to make commercials, although I haven't for years now, but when I did I loved it. Just shooting was so enjoyable, particularly shooting without responsibility . . . having access to an unlimited number of toys which you can move around. I've never had to do commercial work to pay the bills although sometimes it's a near thing and you kid yourself that you're loving it.

When you're an experienced director you shoot cover. If you have a bad actor you do staging in such a way that you play *off* them rather than on them. If you have a scene where you start with a room and people walk into it and then you shoot your close-ups, if you then edit it and start with a

close-up and *then* move out, the scene simply means something different. Every shot sets up different expectations in the audience's head. The shot of a room sets up different expectations. So if you feel you're not getting much from the eyes of a particular actor you try another way. In some ways scripts don't matter at all. A script is not a film in the same way that a landscape isn't a picture.

The process of film-making is extremely unpleasant, but that's not to say it isn't addictive. Spielberg once said that he loved making films but found the process of shooting unpleasant. He said nobody actually believes you when you say it, but he said he hated it and being a producer enabled him to have the pleasure of making films without the agony of the six o'clock call every day. The unpleasantness is really to do with the time pressure. This might sound like an old man talking, but it used to be easier when it was cheaper because the 'electricity' coming from the organization was less ferocious. The early films I made cost maybe 100,000 pounds. Now they cost, I don't know, 18 million? When you start shooting it's like getting on a train and you can't get off.

I have a fairly strong sense of structure and I'm aware that you often have to go slow, quick, slow, quick. I heard it said once that movies should be like a circus with a variety of acts so that what you're hurling at the audience is different kinds of experience. What people want from the movies is thrills. Not necessarily guns or special effects, but *surprises*. It seems more important now that people should enjoy the bits. So many really popular films have three or four memorable *bits* even if the film as a whole isn't actually that good.

You always have to be aware that you're not shooting a sequence, you're shooting a film. You can go into rushes and everybody adores the scene, but you know in your heart of hearts that, OK it's great, but it's actually going to kill the next scene. So that's the anxiety. You have to jump into that pond and swim around in it for three months. When it works it's the most thrilling thing there is. When it doesn't, it's agony.

Barry Norman
Writer and broadcaster

I can remember as a kid going quite often to Ealing Studios
with my old man, who was a producer and director. He
produced *The Cruel Sea* and directed *Dunkirk*, *The Long and
the Short and the Tall* and various other films. So far as I
was concerned, growing up in the film industry was nothing
unusual. I was never star-struck. I think that's a great advantage in the job I do. I've yet to see a movie star walk on water.
They're just like you and me, only prettier.

I used to haunt the cinema on Sunday afternoons when they
had a double bill of oldies. It was a great place for picking up
girls. Basically the cinema is about sex. There you are, fifteen
years old, looking for adventure, randy as hell, sitting in the
dark and there's this girl sitting next to you who obviously
feels pretty much the same. It was terrific. I've given that up.

I've made at least thirty-five 50-minute documentaries about
the film industry and it's now clear to me that you're always
going to get your most interesting stuff from the directors,
writers and producers, and the most tedious stuff from the
stars. For a while I thought this was because movie stars were
stupid. But I can now see it's because they've got a kind of
tunnel vision. It's so competitive. For every star there are a
hundred kids who want his or her job. They're worried about
that.

You can't discuss concepts with stars. You can discuss
specific films and they'll bend your ear for hours. I went to
interview Glenn Ford and we were talking about *Gilda*, which
he made with Rita Hayworth. He was quite interesting on the

film and how it was made and how he was madly in love with Rita Hayworth.

At the end of talking about *Gilda*, I said, 'I'm glad we touched on that subject because I'd like to go on to talk about "film noir".' He said, 'What?' I said, 'Film noir.' He said, 'What's that?' I said, 'Well, in the late forties when you were making *Gilda* everyone was making film noir. *Gilda* was film noir.' He said, 'No, because after *Gilda* I made a comedy.' And that is absolutely typical of the movie star's mentality. Film noir had completely passed him by.

There's a big difference between actors and film stars. Beverly Hills is a village for movie stars. British actors live in Shepherd's Bush next to milkmen or tax collectors. They know what life's about. I make a point of not getting too close to movie stars because if they've made a bad movie I don't feel as though I'm betraying a friend if I criticize it. There are some I think of as friends – Clint Eastwood, Michael Caine, Roger Moore and Sean Connery. But generally movie stars have no interest in you because the whole centre of their existence is what they're doing.

In many ways the film industry is a classless society. Michael Caine and Bob Hoskins are out-and-out Cockneys, but they're big international stars. I suppose until pop music took off it was the only way to get away from your background and into a higher stratum of life.

I reckon seven out of ten films are not worth bothering with. Maybe 20 per cent are OK and if you're very lucky 10 per cent make up for the dross. After all this time, I still go to a movie hoping that this one is going to be the one that makes up for all the dross. I'd pack up the job tomorrow if I lost that.

Ronald Harwood

Screenwriter and playwright: 'The Dresser' etc.

We were in the middle of talking – Sandy Mackendrick, Elmo Williams and I – in a big office in Soho Square and a cable came through from Darryl Zanuck. It was long and detailed but the essence of it was that, in the middle of the script of *High Wind in Jamaica*, the pirates go to an island where they sell their wares and it's run by a kind of pirate king.

The cable said we should change the pirate king to a woman because Lila Kedrova had just won the Academy Award for *Zorba the Greek*. He wanted her to play that woman – he was willing to pay her a lot of money – because he had to face his shareholders the following Monday and he wanted to be able to tell them that he had Lila Kedrova in the part. This was Tuesday and he wanted her to have the new script by Friday.

This was my first big movie. I looked at Sandy for guidance and he just nodded imperceptibly. So I said, 'Yes, yes, I think that's possible.' I said I'd need some typing help. They said fine. Sandy said not to worry, he'd come in and help with it. We'd start on Tuesday evening at 6 p.m., we'd have a relay of secretaries and finish by noon on Wednesday. I went in at 6 p.m. – no Mackendrick. So I sat down and re-wrote it myself. I finished the following evening. I was up twenty-four hours. Then they had that bit re-written – quite rightly, because it was absolutely awful.

As a kind of reward for my willingness and enthusiasm Zanuck's office called me and asked if I'd like to re-write a film called *Rapture*, which was filming in France on the headland opposite to the one where he was filming *The Longest Day*.

I flew across to France. He paid me 200 pounds a day, a fortune for someone like me. I started to re-write and went up on to the headland to watch them filming. Suddenly the sound man took off his earphones – they were in the middle of a scene – and he said, 'C'est Zanuck!' It went round the unit – 'C'est Zanuck! C'est Zanuck!' We all looked up at the sky and a helicopter came over the headland and dropped down. The door opened and out of it got Darryl F. Zanuck. First his cigar, which was very long, and then this very tiny man.

He said, 'C'mon, I want the director and the writer.' We were terrified. We charged off after him into a kind of prefab hut. He said, 'Lemme see the pages.' We gave him fifteen

pages I'd rewritten by then and he went through them two seconds a page and said, 'Fine.' Then he climbed into his helicopter and went back to *The Longest Day*. That was the only time I ever saw him.

On one of my first visits to Hollywood I stayed at the Beverly Hills Hotel at the film company's expense and I fixed up some tennis lessons with the pro at the hotel – fifty bucks an hour in those days. When I got the bill I wanted to pay cash because it was my personal expense. A couple of weeks later I got a letter from the head office of the movie company asking why I'd paid cash for that. I wrote a letter explaining what I'd done and I got back a telegram saying, 'Are you crazy? Charge *everything* to the company.'

The real difference between the theatre and cinema is that the writer is more in control in the theatre. They can't change a line without your permission, whereas in the movies they can. The making of *The Dresser* was unique in my experience because Peter Yates and I were left totally in charge. No one interfered from head office at all. I don't think they realized it would be the success it was. They were very supportive and encouraging. Peter wouldn't change anything without actually calling me. When I was away one weekend trying to find a small house in France he got into a panic and sent an urgent message that I should be there on the Monday morning. When I got to Pinewood I said, 'What's up? Are we behind?' Eventually I found Peter and he said, 'Ronnie, what do you think we should have on the T-shirts?'

In the early sixties I was asked to do some work on a film with Tony Curtis and Zsa Zsa Gabor called *Drop Dead Darling*. Ken Hughes and I were invited over to meet Tony at his suite at the Dorchester. We went in and there was Zsa Zsa Gabor. Ken introduced us and she said, 'Oh darling, you are so wonderful. You must give me some more jokes.' With that we parted and went up to Tony's suite. He was charming. He had a Beatles cap on and was smoking a big Monte Cristo Number Three. I stupidly said, 'Oh, we've just met Zsa Zsa

down there.' I was rather star impressed, you see. He said, 'Oh yeah? What did she want?' So I reported the conversation. He said, 'What?' His face changed and he became quite monstrous. He said, 'I'm not having that f——g bitch interfering in this f——g movie! Get me Ray Stark in Hollywood!' He made his secretary take notes as he was shouting at Ray. I was so alarmed. Eventually he put the phone down and told his secretary to read back what Ray had said. So she said:
'TONY: This f——g bitch must not interfere anymore in this f——g picture!
RAY: I understand that, Tony.
TONY: I'm not having any more of her f——g interfering!'

I'm afraid it got rather blurred there, but that didn't satisfy Curtis. He started to pace up and down and said, 'We're gonna go over and see that f——g bitch. I'm gonna confront her *now!*' He found out she was staying at Claridges and got the car ready. I had my only suit on in those days – what I used to call my audition suit. We went out and there was a huge mob of kids at the front door of the Dorchester. As we were pushing our way through Curtis grabbed me as a shield and I was beaten and bashed. When I regained my balance I was on the bottom of the motor car – a big, long wheelbase Mercedes – and all the buttons of my suit had been torn off. I said to him rather sheepishly, 'All the buttons have gone.' He said, 'Yeah. Tough.' Anyway we got to Claridges and went up to her suite. Just outside the door he butted his Monte Cristo Number Three as you might a cigarette, put it on the radiator and we went in. Now Tony and Zsa Zsa are both Hungarian originally and he tore her off in Hungarian. Ken and I didn't know what was being said. She kept turning to us and saying, 'He's saying such terrible things to me, darling. Terrible things.' When he'd finished out we came, he took up his cigar and we came back. That night she found out my number and telephoned me at home. She said, 'Oh darling, secretly you must write me some . . . ' I said, 'I'm having nothing more to do with it.' And I didn't.

Steve Abbott

Producer: 'A Fish Called Wanda' and others.
Director of Prominent Features

I grew up in a house with no books at all. My dad worked as a cutter in a clothing factory, my mum worked in a shop. When I went up to Cambridge I hadn't even got English Literature O level. I'd never read a book or seen a film other than, say, James Bond, or been to the theatre.

I started out as a chartered accountant. I had thought there was this mystique about being a film producer, but I realized I could learn as I went along. Before setting up Prominent I'd spent a couple of years working with Gilliam on *Munchausen*, Cleese on *A Fish Called Wanda* and Terry Jones on *Erik the Viking*. When we announced Prominent we didn't put any money into it, just subscribed for 1,000 pounds' worth of shares each. Basically the five Pythons (excluding Graham Chapman), myself and Anne James just formed it.

There are two main problems with the set-up, which is probably going to be true of any creative situation: egos and competition. Although the Pythons are all equal partners in Prominent, they're all jealously guarding their own interests and slightly envious if another has more success. There's also the problem of sharing time, although I think in their saner, sober moments they realize that most groups in the entertainment business fall out in no time at all, so it's kind of unique that twenty years on there are no writs flying around.

It's a horrible world in Hollywood. I could never work there. It's a sausage factory, a place where you're feeding a studio system that has to distribute so many films a year, has a production department and has to green light x films a year.

We've never worked like that. When I get to L.A. I hire a car, the cheapest category. Normally I stay with friends or sleep in people's spare rooms or floors. I can have a trip to L.A. for 1,000 pounds all-in, including spending-money and travel. Even though the money will roll in I don't feel the need to be extravagant. But if I'm meeting someone for the first time I make sure they don't see that I've got an Alamo rent-a-car, smallest grade, which cost a third of a Hertz full-size one. It's pathetic but you've got to do it out there.

Betsy Blair

Actress: 'The Snake Pit', 'Marty' etc.

I was offered starlet contracts at seventeen, but I was terribly arrogant at that age. I'd discovered New York and art and politics and the world. I was full of ideals. Then I fell in love with Gene Kelly, who was the choreographer at the Diamond Horseshoe, which was my nightclub job. We married when Gene got his contract to go to Hollywood, so I went with him.

I did four or five movies before *The Snake Pit*. I worked like a demon preparing myself for that part. I made the screen test and Anatole Litvak said, 'Good, now do it making animal noises.' That was when I realized how important it was to be prepared. I *could* do it making animal noises. I got the part and all the critics noticed me.

Anatole Litvak had white hair and white eyebrows. He was very pale. You'd see him next to the camera like some kind of ghost. He never said much. He did many, many takes but never said why. One day, he did talk to Olivia de Havilland. It turned out that she had disagreed with him. The scene went on and on and on – up to sixty takes. At the end I asked Olivia what she did if she disagreed with the director. She said, 'The director is king. You have to go along with what he says. But he has twenty takes *my* way.'

When there's an emotional scene, not only do you have this subliminal relationship with the director, but you're also involved with the lighting cameraman. If you've done a couple of takes, he comes forward with the light meter. That moment is a revelation of how you separate yourself. You stay in your character, but you're perfectly aware of this man coming, and there's a kind of companionship. He's also aware that you're in character, and you hold still. I've always found in both dancing and acting, there's an element of 'game' which I love. It's the challenge; like you have to do this *now*. When you're at home, studying your lines, you can do anything. When you're doing it in your head, silently, the emotion floods into you and the tears come. There's no difficulty at all. But the challenge of recreating all that is fun.

When *Marty* eventually came along I got to read for the girl – they didn't make screen tests because it was a low budget film – and after about the third line someone said, 'I think you've got the part because there was a tear in the eye of Old Stoneface.' That was Burt Lancaster, who was one of the producers. But before I could actually get the part, I was expected to write a letter saying I had been duped and misled into political activity. I couldn't bring myself to do it.

Four years before *Marty* the whole political thing had come to a head. A journalist called me on a Sunday and told me I was going to be fired from *Fine Lady* because I'd spoken sympathetically about all the actors who were being attacked as 'pinkos'. But Gene arranged a meeting for me with L. B. Mayer, which turned out to be the high point of my studio experience.

I was never chased around desks – probably because I was married to Gene Kelly – but also because I was a passionate, serious, left-wing kind of person.

Mayer said, 'You've got a wonderful husband, a wonderful child. What do you want? You've got America.' I was in there so long that Gene came up to the office.

Mayer took us out to the anteroom, put his arm around both of us and said, 'Well, Gene, she's a fine girl, as American as you and me.' As he walked away Gene said, 'You must have given an Academy performance in there.'

So I finished *Fine Lady* and *then* I was blacklisted. My attitude was that I didn't need them. I had a successful husband, so I figured I'd go off and do something else. I was blacklisted for four years but my life went on.

Then the part in *Marty* came up. Gene, who was in the middle of a big musical, went to the head of Metro and said, 'Look, you know she's not going to overthrow the country. Besides, if she doesn't get the part I'm going to quit shooting.' So I was cleared. We had a wonderful time making that movie.

I think we had the best of everything at that time. Gene had been a poor kid; there he was with a nice house on Rodeo Drive. He still lives in it. Every Saturday night we had a party and played charades. People like Judy Garland and George Gershwin came and sang and played. On Sunday we played volleyball in the garden, had dinner and ran a movie. It was a hardworking, full life.

Beverly Hills was still a village. It didn't have any parking meters. Rodeo Drive was where the hardware store was, not where Giorgio was. The atmosphere was so productive and all the people were fulfilled.

Gene was serious. He was very well-educated; he'd studied history at the University of Pittsburgh. He was smart and talented but he was also sexy. Many of the things he did – the dancing with the little cartoon mouse, the alter ego number, were really his concepts. He was a great dancer and a wonderful actor.

At that time I thought there were two kinds of movie star: actors like Spencer Tracy and 'movie stars'. That was another part of my youth and arrogance because I now realize that Gary Cooper was very good. *Real* movie stars do actually have a special quality that makes them movie stars. It isn't just by luck or chance or hype that they're famous.

I now have this feeling of the romance of the studio, the smell of the greasepaint, the little bungalows. The studios were heaven.

Terence Stamp

Actor: 'Billy Budd', 'The Collector', 'Modesty Blaise',
'Far from the Madding Crowd', 'Superman', 'The Hit',
'Superman II', 'Wall Street' etc.

The director who loves you is a luxury. But certainly the
directors for whom I've produced my best work are the ones
I felt really loved me and appreciated me. The whole business
of filming is unnerving, but if the director thinks a lot of you,
it's a kind of protection – against your own fears, against all
the things that can go wrong while the camera's turning.
Wyler made me feel that it was really something for him when
I walked on set. He would come up and say, 'How do you
think we should stage this?' It gave me confidence and made
me feel we were conspirators, that we were in it together. You
can't help but give your best.

Fellini, too, makes you believe he loves you and he demands
you love him. With Fellini I broke through my fear about
filming. You work with fear for so long, you assume you're
not performing your best if you don't feel it. It's like the first
time you eat chilli, it hurts you; then you get used to the hurt,
then you don't want anything without chilli. But working
with Fellini made me realize I could do better work feeling
good and enjoying it. I didn't need the fear anymore.

To me, stage acting was just an aberration. I had no training
for films, but on my first day filming I instinctively felt I'd
come home – that this was my medium, that the camera was
my girl. I followed my intuition.

I just read the script a lot to get insights into the character;
you're looking at someone else's creation and it's your job to
make it believable, to make it work. When the writer hasn't
got it right, you have to bridge the gap.

The best acting is invisible – in a way it's non-existent. Most actors don't know how they do it. I don't know how I do it. But I do know that all performing is to do with energy. Your energy has to be big enough, or compact enough, to hold the attention of the camera – and the audience. The gathering and giving off of energy is more dynamic on film because it's just one minute or thirty seconds. You can be waiting around all day just to do your thirty seconds. I find I have to be careful what I'm doing while I'm waiting; if I'm entertaining the crew, chatting up girls and so on and it comes to the moment, you can find your gumption's gone, the battery's flat. This is why a lot of actors stay ensconced in their caravans; they're not anti-social, they're keeping their energy together, to themselves. I'm looking forward to directing. As an actor

on set it's easy to see how it could be better sometimes, but you can't go around directing other actors when you're an actor – they and the director would resent it. It will be nice to do it officially.

For fifteen years I was content to be part of the director's vision, to do what I was told to do; but for the last ten years I've been working for directors where I feel their vision has nothing to do with mine. You very rarely get a script which is anywhere near how you feel about life. The main thing about moving into directing is I can start putting my own energy into it instead of just being part of it. Making movies is the most fun thing I can think of to do for a living. The movie experience is adventurous – like building a yacht and sailing somewhere – it's a real adventure. That's the glamour of it – because of the pressure, the speed, where you go and the camera. It's life with the boring bits cut out – it's enhanced. But it's also a chance to see life as it really is. One isn't aware of life being enhanced because one hasn't the concentration; but when you go into a cinema, you're sitting in the dark and watching something bigger than you, you bring to it a different quality of awareness that you slide down from when you come back into life. In that sense, I feel I've learned something about my life from movies.

The thing about the camera is that it likes honesty. Some great stage actors pretend they're not photogenic but that's not true – it's the camera not liking exaggeration. You need to be real and honest for the camera to come across – it doesn't like you lying to it. It's like another person, but a rare person – one who's looking for the best in you.

Stephen Frears

Director: 'Gumshoe', 'My Beautiful Laundrette', 'The Hit', 'Sammy and Rosie Get Laid', 'Dangerous Liaisons'

I remember when I first started, I used to leave vital things out. One time, I shot this scene where a man comes into the room holding a gun, but I only used a close-up and people said, 'What's happening here?' 'He's holding a gun', I said. 'But we can't see it.' I knew the man had a gun, so I just assumed everyone else knew. I didn't understand how the camera isolates things.

Later on, I had a different problem with guns. When I was making *The Hit*, people kept coming up to me and saying 'What kind of guns do you want them to use?' and 'How do you want him to die?' I thought, 'Jesus, why are they asking me? I'm much too sensitive to be asked these sorts of things.' Then I realized that's where the fun lay, so I designed the killing in the garage. I worked it all out and it just came right. But I didn't know before then that that was what you were supposed to do as a director. I thought other people did it. I just believed what I saw – I think it's sort of a failure of curiosity.

When I started, I had to edit scenes just to make them work at all. Now I shoot them so they work and the editing is much more complex; you're using it to get the meaning you want and isolate it. But for years, it was just the panic of thinking, 'Have we got a scene? Is it any good?' I couldn't believe I was doing it. I was unprepared for being a creative person.

You'd have thought making *Liaisons* would be a great jump for me, but it wasn't at all. It didn't feel that different because the material was so good. The trouble starts when the script is intractable and doughy so you can't get any spark out of it. When it comes to life, you can deal with anything; but, if the scene doesn't work, the troubles of the world are on your shoulders. If there's no life, there isn't a film. If you're doubtful, you can cover it up with sleight of hand but you feel found out in some way.

Time and the movement of the light are both very important – the light changes all the time. I've become rather good at shaping the day to get the best from it. If you lose control, the spending and the schedule go out. Dealing with the money and dealing with the world is part of the job. It's not necessarily creative in a painterly way, but it's part of the process. If you can't deal with that side of things, you can have a lot of trouble.

I've become adroit at juggling. I discovered you could do a scene in one shot. Of course, Orson Welles did this so effectively at the beginning of *Touch of Evil*. Apparently, there was only half an hour of shooting time left and they'd shot absolutely nothing all day. And then he did that long, long take – and suddenly they were two days ahead of schedule!

On *Liaisons*, I found the decision to cast American actors very liberating. It was like putting an axe to the past. I didn't want to make a kind of Royal Shakespeare version of it – and I was hired for that very reason. Christopher Hampton was asked why he wanted me and he said, 'Because he won't respect it. Because he'll be irreverent.' I suspect my version of *Liaisons* is probably rather naff.

I think I'm irreverent because I get bored easily. It's an English thing – if confronted by Art, the instinct is to be very Philistine and, confronted by Philistinism, you become extremely sensitive. It's like that song in a Marx Brothers film – 'Whatever it is, I'm against it'. That's very much my attitude. It means you start trying new and different ways of doing things – like playing variations on a theme – to entertain yourself. You know, Hitchcock used to get very bored on set. He'd sit there telling stories and the work just wouldn't get

Not all Stephen's movies have naked Michelle Pfeiffer in them...

pity...

location shooting in L.A. for "GRIFTERS": directed by Stephen Frears

done – though, of course, he'd done it all in his head.

What's so peculiar to me about directing is that it is like a craft – just like woodcutting or making furniture. I think of myself, not as a technician, but as a craftsman. It surprises me. You have a strong sense of making something with your hands even though your hands touch nothing.

It's like an education, a continuing analysis for me. I make a film and then spend a lot of time thinking about it afterwards. I make it and then gradually discover what I've done. It's like automatic writing – it's intuitive. I always have the writer on set. They seem to have a sort of analytical intelligence that I don't. I just tease out the meaning as I see it, then check with the writer that I'm doing it right – that it's consistent.

When it's going well, the pressure is wonderful. You're like a conductor. When the material's alive you can orchestrate it; you can set the pitch and the tone and the emphases.

At work you make so many decisions; but at home people take the piss out of you. No one listens to you in the same way. It's very, very hard. You go from being this ordinary bloke to being this man who's given this tremendous authority – you're in charge.

Catherine Wyler

Producer: 'The Memphis Belle'

My movie début was in my father's *The Best Years of Our Lives*. I played a kid sitting in a drug store when Dana Andrews walks in. I had a terrific crush on him, and you can see me staring at him with my mouth open.

When I was a kid I'd see my father going over scripts at all hours of night, sitting at his desk working in a pool of light. I always thought of him as going into this long tunnel. It became a total obsession for him, to the exclusion of everything else for months at a time. My mother said it was as if he was submerged a few feet under water. Sometimes he was amiable, sometimes he was irascible – but mostly he wasn't there.

There were three stages. During the pre-production stage it was like normal nine-to-five life. He'd come home and talk about the script problems or whatever at the dinner table. The great thing about movies is that everybody can have an opinion, however uninformed, and we all did. We learned a lot.

During production he was totally gone. Then, at the editing stage, it would be once again more like normal life. Then he'd hang around with us, and there would be three months of fun and games. I always thought it would be a great life.

He did produce some films as well as direct them, but he believed – and I share this – that it's the collaborative effort, the friction, that makes a movie better. For example, a writer and a director are better than a writer/director. He did his best work when he had a producer to fight with.

My first job was as a gofer (runner). Then I became a story

editor: I decided those dinner table conversations ought to be worth something. I knew something about plot, and I liked writers. I started with Ray Stark, then I worked for Joe Levine. Then I had children and went to Washington, where I discovered the whole other world of independent film-making. So I thought I could do that.

I was attracted to this project (*Memphis Belle*) because it was in the family attic. My father flew on five missions to get the footage and made this 16mm documentary about a Flying Fortress – a wartime propaganda picture. Everybody on my

picture learned from it and stole from it, and I know he'd appreciate that. It's an *hommage*.

When I decided to do it, the first person I called was my uncle, my mother's brother, who owns a B-17 Flying Fortress. I said, if you play your cards right your plane can be the Memphis Belle. So it's even more of a family occasion.

TV may reach more people, but movies are much more powerful. My father liked making – dirty word – 'message' pictures. He made a pacifist movie, *The Friendly Persuasion*; he made an anti-western western about the silliness of the macho image, *The Big Country*. He made some movies which were pure fun, like *Roman Holiday*. He made *The Best Years of Our Lives*, which was about how a country is living at a particular time. I'd love to make something like that right now – then you hit a response, a chord, in the audience. And that's got to be the best.

Mrs Miniver also hit the audience, but that was more of a propaganda picture. He strongly wanted America to lean towards Britain because at that time America still had not entered the war.

He believed that making movies was a craft. He didn't get into any contortions about art. You're setting out to tell a good story, to entertain, and if it ends up making people think, that's terrific.

People believe that making movies is glamorous, but they don't know that you're in the dark all the time. You're in sound studios and editing rooms and dubbing rooms – these little black boxes. If you're working in the winter it's dark when you go to work and dark when you come out. Then the movies are seen in the dark.

There's so much going on, on so many levels – to get it all right, to keep it all moving. It changes all the time, it's constantly renewing itself. It's organized chaos. It's so absorbing; it's creating a whole world.

Richard Griffiths

Actor: 'Gandhi', 'Gorky Park', 'Greystoke: The Legend of Tarzan' etc.

When I was filming *Gorky Park* in Finland (which was pretending to be Russia), it was so cold there was a fountain that had actually frozen solid in mid-spray. We were working in about 30 below – it was so cold it couldn't snow. They had to ship snow in from 200 miles away. Sixty tons, four truckloads – enough to cover the whole square two inches deep. That's the essence of movies. We filmed for six hours and then had to clear the snow away, because the Finns didn't want snow.

I did a thing called *Prisoners of Conscience* for the Beeb, which was set in Santiago, in Chile and Rio. 'Are we going to Chile?' I said. 'Well, no,' they said, 'but we are going on location – to Reigate.' The BBC has a secret map of Greater London and the South East and on this map there are streets which have coloured ribbons attached to them and flags which say, 'Very like Lisbon', 'Madrid', 'Santiago', 'Zagreb' etc. The city which most looks like Moscow, apart from Moscow, is Dundee.

For the funeral scene in *Gandhi*, they circulated all the clubs, societies and teams in Delhi and said, we'd like you to come along and be part of the crowd. They couldn't pay individual people but they told the clubs they'd give their members two rupees each as a donation towards club funds. They figured there'd be between 20 and 50,000 of them. They also put up bills and stickers throughout Delhi and the general gossip and TV/radio exposure gave them cause to believe that 200,000 people might turn up. As a consequence, catering was required to engage fifty water tankers to give the crowd water.

On the day it was half a million people so there was only water for half of them . . .

During the first take of the funeral scene, the head fell off the mannequin of Gandhi, which meant they couldn't use it, so they asked Ben Kingsley if he'd be prepared to be dead for the afternoon – in the blazing heat. He had to lie there not moving. So in the movie when you see him dead, that's Ben. They couldn't fake it.

The only thing that's REAL on this set is me – and I'm not too sure about that by now..

FAKE snow

Kitty Carlisle Hart

Singer and actress

I came from a middle-class New Orleans family. My father
was a doctor. We weren't rich, but in New Orleans you had
a maid and a cook. My parents were both poor when they
married, but then my father got to be very well known. When
I married Moss Hart in 1946 I said to him, 'Which is better,
to be poor like you were when everyone around you is poor,
or to be poor like we were when everyone around you is rich?'
I think it was worse for us because we were always pretending.
We had to be in the right place at the right time in order to
meet the right people, so we always had the worst room at
the best hotel.

I went to Hollywood in 1934 to do *Murder at the Vanities*.
My mother was delighted for me, but she hated Hollywood.
It was an environment where everyone important she had no
respect for. I was frightened, of course, as most people were.
In those days they were gathering up anybody who could sing
because they were making all those musicals, so any girl who
could sing and looked nice went to Hollywood to be in the
movies.

My mother gave no quarter to Hollywood. We lived in the
Beverly Wilshire Hotel. She wore the little black hat with the
veil and white gloves and made no concessions whatsoever. I
wasn't allowed to go out with anyone that we had not met
socially so I didn't go anywhere. I didn't know anybody. My
mother played bridge. My big excitement was watching her
play bridge on a Saturday night and bringing my knitting. It
wasn't much fun.

They put me in a costume in the early days of *Murder at the Vanities*, a South Sea Island number. All the girls were lying on their backs with feathered fans and I was supposed to come out of the sea like a nymph. I wore three velvet fig leaves and I called my mother and said, 'I can't come out of the dressing-room, I'm afraid. I look so naked. Come quick!' She came over and said, 'This will not do.' We went to the front office and made a pact that I would do the scene, but I wouldn't pose for still photographs in this very naked costume.

In those days there were no unions and I can remember sometimes working for thirty-six hours at a time. I knew very little of Hollywood in those days. It was a lovely town – no smog – you could ride horses down the middle of Sunset Boulevard. Years later I realized why I didn't make it in movies – I wasn't very good!

I was slumming in *A Night at the Opera*. I did it because Paramount were through with me and they rented me out. I also wanted to sing opera seriously. The first day on the set I was singing an aria from Trovatore and there was a facsimile of the Metropolitan Opera. I wasn't happy with the first take. We started again, but stopped when I realized the playback wasn't my voice. The director told me to just do it and he'd explain later. I was so upset and bewildered. I walked off the set and called my agent. Apparently they didn't trust me to sing the operatic sequences as well as a real opera singer, so they'd gone to New York and recorded two opera singers from the Met. I was supposed to do the playback for Rosa Ponselle's voice. I cried and cried and said I didn't want to do it. The movie was held up for three days until Irving Thalberg called me and I wept all over his office. Finally he agreed to let me sing, so when I now hear that high 'C' in the Miserere I know it's mine!

When we did movies we tried to look as nice and tidy as we could. If you had a lapel that went the wrong way somebody would always come up and fix it for you. Now all the actors and actresses try to look as messy as they possibly can.

I think it's really quite unattractive. Actors are now no longer controlled financially by the studios, which is very good. In other words they get a piece of the action. I could certainly have done with a piece of *A Night at the Opera*. I'm told it's playing somewhere in the world every day of the year.

I loved 'A NIGHT at the OPERA' - but which MARX brother were you?

John Guare

Playwright and screenwriter: 'Atlantic City USA',
'Taking Off'

In some ways, writing a movie is like working on a musical. You have very many scenes, very many locations. In a musical there are certain things you can't write because the music takes care of that; in a movie there are certain things you underwrite because the camera will take care of that.

I worked on *Taking Off* with Milos Forman. That was divine. At that time Milos didn't let actors see the script. He would recite it to them and then they'd try to repeat it back to him while the cameras were rolling. Then he'd say, 'Cut – print it. That's fine.' Then he'd say the next line to them. It made the actors very vulnerable because they didn't know what they were going to say. It was quite extraordinary – he didn't even tell them what the scene was about. I can't imagine that he still works like that. He couldn't.

I also wrote the script of *Atlantic City* for Louis Malle. The great thing about Louis is that he uses the camera like a novelist. *Atlantic City* had to be shot in the real place, because it depended on the story being played against a documentary reality.

If it hadn't been for Louis, the producers would have kept changing the script. I had written a line, 'You should have seen the Atlantic Ocean in the old days.' Meaning – everything has changed now. But the producers had a fit. They said, 'Surely you meant "You should have seen Atlantic *City* in the old days", because an ocean can't change. Don't you understand? We'll be laughed at!'

That's an example of what producers can do. In the movies,

producers own the copyright. It's a property – that's what it literally means. They can do what they want; they can bring in other writers to write key scenes or make a happy ending. In the theatre the writer has control – over cast, decor, director. It's a key difference – you own your own work. In movies, the writer has no control. Ring Lardner Jr has written fifteen scripts that were never made. That's a life's work!

I grew up loving movies. My uncle, Billy Grady, was Head of Casting at MGM. A horrible man, horrible. Before that he'd been a very powerful agent – he'd represented Al Jolson, W. C. Fields, Will Rogers, Marilyn Miller. He'd discovered Jimmy Stewart. He's the one who wrote the memo about Fred Astaire's first screen test: 'Can't act, can't sing, can dance a little.' My uncle died at the motion picture home, sharing a breathing machine with Bruce Cabot, Virginia Bruce and Mary Astor.

Peter Yates

Director: 'Bullitt', 'The Dresser' etc.

Originally I thought, Why bother to be a director, when I'd never be as good as David Lean? But I've since discovered there's room for other people as well.

I started as an actor, not a very good one. Then I raced cars for a bit. I began working in films as an assistant director to Tony Richardson and various other directors. Then I made three films in England – *Summer Holiday*, *Robbery* and *One Way Pendulum*, and from that I was offered *Bullitt* in America.

I was the first British director to be asked to do a big action movie of that kind. Steve McQueen felt that he was a bit of a pioneer in hiring me. The studio was delighted because they were trying to get him off the lot, and they thought if he was stupid enough to take on an English director of an action film they'd be bound to get rid of him.

We had to decide whether to make it in the studio – which was the accepted way of making films at that time – or on location. I knew more about making a film on location than they did, so I opted for making it entirely on location in San Francisco. I only discovered later that McQueen had a very bad reputation – I think that because I spoke with an English accent he thought I was far more intelligent than I was. He listened to me, and I've since been told he wasn't exactly known for that.

We both loved cars. It was the first film to use the principal actor in the car chase itself. Steve and I both admired the skill of driving rather than just the feeling of a destruction derby.

We were much more interested in cars just missing than hitting each other. We only destroyed one car and that was the car that hit the petrol station at the end of the chase.

I didn't find McQueen difficult. I try to create an atmosphere where actors can work; a director needn't necessarily enforce his ego on other people's ideas. A lot of people on both sides of the camera, producers, directors and actors, are inclined to have enormous egos which do get in the way of creating anything worthwhile. I think that if Puttnam, when he was in America, had kept his mouth shut he would have done much better.

Editing is fun, if only because you don't have to get up before nine in the morning. It's a wonderful, relaxing time, a time when you can change things and be inventive. I love the mixing period too, when everything starts to come together. The hardest time is when you're shooting.

These days you have to translate the story more than they used to. Thank God the days of the master shot, the two-shot, then the over-the-shoulder, are now over. I haven't done a master shot for years.

You're always up against schedules. That's why it's helpful having been an A.D., because you know the language of the production office. If you need to give yourself a bit of freedom now and again, if you're getting into a scene that you feel may develop, then you can wangle yourself a bit more time without them realizing. That's when it helps to be English in America. They can't ever believe that you're not being completely and utterly honest. They haven't learnt about English deviousness yet.

Where did he learn Deviousness?

Jeremy Thomas
Producer: 'The Last Emperor' and many others

My dad, Ralph Thomas, was a movie director – he did the *Doctor in the House* films and many others – so I grew up in movies. I made my own first movie in Dirk Bogarde's house when I was thirteen. I borrowed my dad's 16mm Bolex. It was called *A Day at the Fishmonger*, and it had a cast of many herrings. Then I did the chariot race from *Ben Hur* with wheelbarrows in the garden.

I'm a show business brat. My uncle Gerald was a film director – he made the 'Carry On' films. Every holiday I'd go and watch the filming; the smells of the stages at Pinewood still bring memories back to me. My parents lived very close to Pinewood; after shooting every day the house would be full of actors. It's not a business you hand over like the family shop, but I picked up a lot.

When I left school at seventeen I went straight into films. I went into film laboratories, then the cutting room. Then I produced my first film, in Australia, when I was twenty-four and I've been doing it ever since. I'm fascinated by movies. It's my hobby, too. I think of life in terms of film.

There can be intense frustration sometimes, when you're doing a film, but it heals up. It's like a relationship with somebody. You can have a bad relationship with someone, but then after two years you're happy to see them again. Those sleepless nights and difficult mornings – you forget them. You think it's all been worth it.

I shall control
WORLD RIGHTS..
I've been directed by
BIGGER FISH
than him ..

John Schlesinger

*Director: 'Darling', 'Midnight Cowboy', 'Far from
the Madding Crowd', 'Sunday, Bloody Sunday' and
many others*

I had a box-Brownie still camera at the age of nine and my
father, who was a great encourager, said if you're going to
take pictures you'd better learn how to develop them. So I did
– in a cupboard under the stairs. Eventually I had a 9.5mm
camera and started to make films and then graduated when I
came out of the army to doing 16mm jobs: granny in the back
garden, the school outing to the seaside. Then I did a film
called *Horror*, which was about a couple of escaped convicts.
The first serious one I did was in my first term at university,
a film about hanging in the seventeenth century. There was
a gibbet near where my family lived on Inkpen Beacon and
we decided to do the story behind it on 16mm. That was in
1948. Then I did another one which was more ambitious and
not as good, a dreadful flop, got blown up to 35mm. Then I
tried to get a job in the film industry.

My first job in the industry was working for Worldwide
Pictures researching a film about British cheese for the Milk
Marketing Board. John Arlott was in it. Then I went into
television. I remember an endless argument with a lady at the
BBC, quite a powerful woman. I used to argue that I was
making films for television. She said you're making *television*.
I couldn't quite see the difference and still can't. To me a film
is a film however it's shown. You may have to keep the camera
closer, grab the audience quicker, simplify the long shots so
the composition is clear on that small screen, but I always
knew I wanted to get into films. I used to ask permission to
borrow films I'd made for the 'Tonight' programme to show

to the Boulting brothers in the hope that I'd get a job, but they wouldn't let me. So I pinched my own work.

You used to be able to make films in this country which could make their money back, and more, here alone. My first film was well into profit just from showing here. You can't do that now. *Sunday, Bloody Sunday* cost two million pounds. It took a long time to shoot. We had to re-cast in the middle. It's more difficult to get things financed now. I don't think it's getting any better. People are very scared. The cost of releasing film now is so huge that it's cheaper to do a risky subject on TV. I would never be able to make *Midnight Cowboy* in the present climate, I'm certain of it. They'd say it was too odd, too downbeat. And we could never have done it for the price we did then.

In films you've really got more control than anywhere else in the entertainment business because you've got the scissors. Time was when the director directed the movie and the cutting was done by other people. You had nothing to do with the editing or the mix or the music. I can't conceive of that. I would hate to be in that situation. I think it's a fairly personal game. There are, of course, cases where things are taken away from you. Things have been cut behind my back or taken out. There was a case in point in *Darling* when it was shown at the Moscow Film Festival where we were greeted by the head of the British film delegation, who wasn't a film-maker. He said they'd seen fit to cut a little bit of my film. I said, 'What!?' He said, 'There's no need to sulk. It doesn't seem to me to make much difference to it.' Well it made a lot of difference as far as I was concerned and I was very angry. It got restored eventually, but not in America. American television censorship is ludicrous, terribly prudent and self-righteous. We had an ironic situation with *Madame Souzatska*. There's one line where the boy is having a terrible quarrel with this teacher and says, 'Fuck your culture.' You can have that in London, you can even have it for the Queen Mother at the royal première. Outside London the only word that is acceptable if it is to be a swear word is 'bugger', which is interesting when you analyse what the two words actually mean.

I think musically very much at an early stage. It's also so pleasurable as part of the film-making process. It's the first time that another artist working on the film is able to surprise you, sometimes unpleasantly so, but more often than not a pleasant surprise at how much enhanced a scene is because of someone else's contribution. Suddenly after months in the cutting-room there's a fresh vision because of someone else's contribution.

I like the editing process. Actually on the floor is so pressured that sometimes it's agony. It depends on the film. My most successful film was one of the least happy to make. It was a miserable shoot. I didn't like the New York crew terribly. I didn't think they were interested in what was going on. I had a Polish cameraman who didn't get on with his crew. There was always something worse going on just off camera on 42nd Street than what we were trying to do on it.

I love working in Hollywood. It's nice to get up when the sun's shining all the time. I rent a home if I'm there for a long time. I don't like Cannes. I like the show, I don't much like the biz. I must say I think Cannes is full of bullshit, although it's a very good marketplace and it is possible to have a film come to light at Cannes if you're an unknown director.

John Mortimer

Novelist, playwright and screenwriter

How did I begin? I did this Punch and Judy show for a friend of my father, and then, when he was put in charge of wartime films, he thought that the lad who'd done the Punch and Judy was just the person to make films to beat Hitler. So I got this job in the Crown Film Unit as a fourth assistant director. I had to say 'Quiet, please' at the beginning of every shot, and I said 'Quiet, please' and nobody took any notice. So I yelled at them, 'Quiet, you bastards!' and they went on strike. I was a disaster.

So they said you won't do so much damage if you're a scriptwriter. I was paid 11 pounds a week and I learned to write film scripts – how to set them out. You had to put in much more detail then: mid-shot, long-shots etc.

The war ended and I became a barrister. Then I wrote a play called *Dock Brief*, and because that was fairly successful I got offers to write films.

When I was first married a man rang up and said would I like to write a film? He had this film studio in Chancery Lane full of cameras, lights, girls typing. And he said would you like to come on safari in South Africa? I said I'd absolutely love to. He said I'll call you next week. He didn't call, so I went back to the film studios and it was totally gone; nothing there except a wholesale greengrocer's. It was like a dream.

Then Anatole de Grunwald took me up. He used to lie on a couch in the Ritz, with his shoes off and holes in his socks, and offer you everything: the world, girls, and riches beyond belief. He'd always offer you something good to do, but before you could do that you'd have to do something awful. I wrote a really terrible film for him, with Susan Hayward and Peter Finch. It was dire.

You can make a perfectly decent living writing films that never get made. The reason for that is that producers can't read books, they can't read anything except scripts. Then they can read a script and decide they don't want to do it anyway. I wrote a lot of scripts that were never made. My score is one script in ten made. It was horrible, I wouldn't do it again. You're a well paid lackey, and you don't see the result of your labours. If you do see it, you sit in some embarrassment in the cinema, hearing lines you never wrote.

Another thing – they always want to change the script in order to get stars. If you make the Major a woman we could get Elizabeth Taylor. Or they'd call a character Cary – for Cary Grant. 'Cary comes in here' – but then of course you wouldn't get Cary.

For me, that's why writing for television is better – it gets done, and they respect you more. Film is not a writer's medium, it is a director's medium.

I went to Hollywood for a while, where I was miserable and lonely. Then I fell into better company. I met Jack Clayton and worked on *The Innocents* (which is *The Turn of the Screw*). That was a very good film. He taught me most of everything I know. How to end a scene and begin the next scene, and so on.

Then I wrote, with Penelope (my first wife), *Bunny Lake is Missing* for Otto Preminger. It all went on at a nursery school in Hampstead. We lived there and our child went to the school. But in order to write it, we had to go to a hotel in Honolulu (because Preminger was there making some film about Pearl Harbor). So there we sat, eating dolphin steaks. There was a hotel pool in which the dolphins used to dance to the Merry Widow waltz, and the ones that couldn't dance got turned into dolphin steaks. Preminger was absolutely ghastly to actors, but perfectly nice to writers.

Then I met Sam Spiegel, and wrote a film that was also never made. I wrote quite a lot on his yacht. He liked to see twenty pages at a time – so you'd take him these twenty pages and it would be wonderful. He said, 'Christ, thank God I've got you. These are the best twenty pages I've ever seen!' Then, overnight, he'd show them to his cleaning-lady, or his lawyer, or his dentist, and by the morning it had become twenty pages of absolute shit. That happened all the time, but he was incredibly generous.

You had to go on this bloody yacht and stay there. He'd cast off in the night and you'd be marooned on it. The yacht would drop anchor outside St Tropez and fifteen girls would get loaded on, and then let off in the morning.

Once I said I wanted a swim. So the yacht – which was about the size of a Channel steamer – stopped and a gangplank was let down. The captain and the crew were standing watching, the steward standing by with clean towels. I walked down into this beautiful clear sea. And suddenly a sailor pulled the plug in the loo and I was absolutely surrounded with floating shit. I think that's a metaphor.

Producers want to see a treatment, which tells you the story, but I only know what the story is when I'm about three-quarters of the way through it. If you put your characters in this sort of straitjacket, they don't have any life. If the characters live, with any luck they'll proceed to do their own thing.

But writing for these people is a very seductive way of life. You never got to an airport but there was a huge black car with a driver, which you could keep. So if you went out to dinner, you had him until you went to bed. You could stay at the Beverly Hills Hotel and buy clothes and put them on the tab.

The trouble with movie producers is that they don't understand the process of writing. They think that one writer is just the same as another. When one dies, they put another one in his place. It's like building the Pyramids.

DOROTHY LAMOUR leaned a great deal on me..
I'm hoping to STAR in a remake of 'A TREE GROWS IN BROOKLYN'..

rood...

Dick Clement & Ian La Frenais

TV and film writers: 'The Likely Lads', 'Porridge', 'Water' and many more

I.L.F.: It was our intention to come here to work on films, but we got locked into a TV situation. That gave us some security for the first year, and also taught us to think and write American.

In TV the frustrations all start when you have the series commissioned, whereas in film all the frustration is *getting* to that point at all. We're writer-producers, and a long time passes between writing a script and trying to get it produced. Fortunately we can fill in that enormous time with TV work; that saves our sanity. You need about six or seven projects, all bubbling.

We know people who live on 'development' – some English guys have come over here whose development deals have enabled them to buy a house and leapfrog over us, financially. But then they may never get anything actually made. At the moment Dick and I have four screenplays out there. One will go very soon, because it's attached to a top director – he's a very successful 'element'; and a friendly one.

D.C.: An element makes a huge difference. If you go in with, say, Tom Hanks, you're ten squares ahead on the board-game before you begin.

I.L.F.: Mind you, everyone goes in saying 'This is a project for Tom Hanks.' It's when you go in saying 'I've *got* Tom Hanks.'

D.C.: – it's like you've already thrown a six to leave 'GO' . . . It drives us crazy. I still feel as if we're camped somewhere outside Fortress Hollywood being ignored, except for the occasions when they pour boiling oil over us.

We actually got to make a film two years ago. It's because you like it so much that you keep going, which also makes you so frustrated. The screenplay is only the blueprint for the building, and you love the moment when there's suddenly all those people putting it up.

I.L.F.: All we want is to be in a small office somewhere, on location, with secretaries turning out tomorrow's call sheets.

It's easier, as there's two of us. He was very depressed two days ago. And then another day it'll be me. It's quite frustrating at the moment. One of our projects seems to be nowhere; one of them – we don't know what's happening to that; one of them, we have a star attached to it but we don't know which studio is going to be interested; and the other one is going to be done next year. Luckily we're working on a TV series and a stage musical for England.

We still feel slightly foreign here. But you don't have to be English to feel foreign in Hollywood. Anyone who hasn't made at least one film here feels alien.

D.C.: For morale's sake, it's easier with two of you. And for working. One of you can have a bad idea, but it can actually create a good one. Even a rotten idea can unclog the works. So we don't stop ourselves mouthing bad ideas.

I.L.F.: Executives are getting younger. At Fox, where the executives are extremely young, we were taking a meeting recently and Dick said to them, 'Now do any of you want to go to the lavatory before we make this pitch?'

D.C.: They sort of laughed . . .

I.L.F.: . . . but it really went over their heads.

D.C.: One of them was so young – they'd just given him a birthday cake and it was made of milk and cookies.

I.L.F.: The worst thing is that a studio doesn't embrace a script, even when it really likes it. It doesn't use its power and muscle to call the big agencies. Instead, it throws it back at you and says, 'Now get a director,' or 'Maybe you should find another element.' It shows that the most important thing in this town is *access*.

D.C.: William Goldman said, 'A good script is one that Robert Redford wants to do. A bad script is one that Robert Redford doesn't want to do.'

Here's a true Hollywood story. Clint Eastwood called Warner Brothers and asked for the name of the guy in charge of a project, because he needed a word with him. They said it's Bill Smith. So Eastwood gets back to the switchboard and asks to be put through. Bill Smith happens to be in his office alone, his secretary's out, so he picks up the phone and says, 'Yeah, who is it?' 'This is Clint Eastwood. I'm looking for Phil Smith.' And he replies, 'Yeah, this is Phil.' He'd changed his name instantly.

I.L.F.: I know it sounds silly, but tennis is the biggest bonus to living here. We can play every day.

Anne Coates

*Film editor: 'The Horse's Mouth', 'Tunes of Glory',
'Lawrence of Arabia' (including the re-issue), 'Murder
on the Orient Express', 'The Elephant Man' and many
others*

When I started cutting I really didn't know that much about
it. The first film I cut was *The Pickwick Papers*, directed by
Noel Langley. He was a first-time director and *he* didn't know
what he was doing either.

Originally I wanted to be a racehorse trainer. But then I
got interested in the movies. There weren't any film schools
in those days; you just had to learn as you worked your way
up. Most of the top directors – David Lean, Charlie Crichton,
the Ealing boys – they'd all come from editing.

And it was a job that women could do. Nowadays they can
be anything – cameramen, assistant directors. Then you could
either be a secretary, a continuity girl or an editor. Not being
in the union, the only place I could get a job was in religious
films. Then eventually I got into the union and moved across
to Pinewood Studios.

There was a lot of excitement in those days: the British film
industry was doing really well. There was Two Cities, there
was Gainsborough Studios and there was Ealing. I was offered
the chance to direct, but by then I was married and had a
child and I don't think it's possible to direct and bring up
children. If you're a director you've got to be there first thing
in the morning to last thing at night – nothing happens if
you're not there.

It's much tougher working in Hollywood than in England.
It's more of a rat race. Generally speaking, the assistants are
not as well trained as in England; they're not so well organized.
The first A.D.s often don't have the same discipline as British

ones; that's why they're asked to come over here to work. Spielberg told me once that British crews are the best in the world.

It took two years to restore *Lawrence of Arabia*. I'd forgotten a lot about it, because when I finish a film I put it out of my head. But when Bob Harris found me – after a long search, because he thought I was in England – it all flooded back. I hadn't seen it for fifteen years. I'd forgotten what a marvellous film it was, because when you're working on something day and night, seven days a week, you get too close to it. Seeing it again was a real experience. I'd forgotten how moving it was, and how funny. Spielberg and Larry Kasdan both said that it was the film which inspired them to go into movies. The funny thing is that it's much more revered here than in England.

I got much more attention this time round. At the time I didn't even come over for the Oscars ceremony. This was because (a) I didn't expect to win, and (b) Sam Spiegel didn't offer to pay or anything, which they do nowadays. My husband and I couldn't afford the trip.

In fact I was away on holiday in Spain at the time. Then I heard I'd won and I went to London Airport to pick up the Oscar. They charged me customs duty on it! I must say, that shook me – to be charged customs duty on a prize! It was because it was gold, or gold-plated. They charged me 15 shillings! The customs people opened it up and looked at it because they'd never seen an Oscar before. I didn't even know if it was going to be the same size as the actors' ones or not. I thought that if you were a technician you only got a little one.

I love working with David Lean. I'm keeping my fingers crossed that *Nostromo* really goes ahead. It keeps being put back. With David, I've always known what he wanted. Most top directors use the same editor every time, because it's a very close relationship. It's always nerve-wracking working with a new director; I'm always terrified when I'm running the first cut. Will they like my style?

I went to a party once. There were about twenty-five people there. They were all living well – nice cars, nice houses. And I was the only one who was actually working! They were all on development deals of one sort or another, or they were maybe writing. But none of them was actually *doing* anything. To my knowledge, about three have done something since then, but the others are still on development deals. I couldn't live like that! My nerves would be in shreds.

Mary-Anne Page

Independent producer: 'Highway to Hell'

My first interview was at Columbia. This guy said, 'Yes, I do have a job. I need someone to do development for Tom Hanks.' So I met Tom's agent that afternoon. The next morning I flew to New York and met his manager. That afternoon I flew to San Francisco and met Tom. And then I had the job. I was very lucky; Columbia had just made the deal with Tom and I happened to walk into this guy's office at the right moment.

I had to read scripts that were submitted to Tom. Mainly, though, I looked for material for him. Then I worked for Ray Stark, doing the same thing but at a slightly higher level. Then, after a couple of other jobs, I became an independent producer. I'm now producing our first film *Highway to Hell*. It's a comedy about a kid going to Hades, with a lot of jokes and special effects, and all the Underworld stuff updated.

The first moment when it all seemed real was when I was sitting in this crummy little building in Hollywood doing all the paperwork. Suddenly this big truck pulls in; it was full of movie equipment. That's the moment it suddenly hit me.

I can't believe – with a film on our small budget – that we're getting directors' chairs with our names on them. When I see those, it'll be embarrassing. But that truck – that was exciting. And when I see the first dailies, that'll be exciting too.

I wanted James Stewart for a cameo role in this movie, playing an old man, Sam, who's in fact an angel. He would've been perfect for that. I read in the paper that he was doing a signing at Brentano's bookstore in Century City. He was

autographing his new book of poems, Tuesday morning at noon. So I put on my dark business suit, went there, and stood in line in the 90-degree heat. I got there at ten, and there were already fifty people in line. I was armed with the script, and tapes of two of our director's films. It's so embarrassing, to even remember it. Finally, when I got to him, I handed him the package and said, 'Mr Stewart-I-enjoyed-your-book-I've-brought-you-a-script-and-two-movies' – I was try-ing to talk very fast, because the line was moving forward – 'I-know-you'll-love-it, please-look-at-the-role-of-Sam, we-very-much-want-you-to-play-it, thank-you-very-much.'

And he said, 'Well thank *you* very much.'

But we didn't get him.

Tony Walton

Film and stage designer: 'All That Jazz', 'The Boy Friend', 'Mary Poppins', 'Murder on the Orient Express', 'A Funny Thing Happened on the Way to the Forum' and many others

When Walt Disney was trying to persuade Julie Andrews (then my wife) to star in *Mary Poppins*, part of the bait was to ask me to design it. Julie and I had a firm rule never to work together, but then she found out she was pregnant and we decided we should be together.

Disney was wonderful to work with. He was much bolder than people realized. People in the studio tended to play it safe, and that drove him bananas. He'd go through the trash cans in the wee hours of the morning, or late at night, and if he found something adventurous he'd stick it back on the drawing board and say 'go with that'.

There was a large team working on the storyboarding, the ideas and so on – it was by no means just me. They were terrific – making models, drafting everything up, making changes. Then it would go into the sausage machine and when it came out it tended to look a bit 'Disneyfied'. For instance, if we'd designed something with an English watercolour flavour, by the time it came to be built and painted it would have moved back to the way Disney things always turned out. And part of this was just 'we know he likes that'. There's an animated sequence where the live characters jump into pictures on the pavement. We'd originally conceived these paintings as naïve and primitive – everything in the sequence was supposed to have this quality – but every time they went into the animation department they came out looking like Dumbo. So I'd say this to Disney and he'd call a meeting and explain it all over again, but gradually it would slide back. In the end there were some elements that remained but it was obviously very frustrating, for him, too.

Another interesting thing about Disney was his home. There was no indication there at all of who he was or what he did – no awards, no Mickeys or Minnies. I made some mention of this to his wife once and she said, 'I remember our daughter, when she was young, reading a Disney comic. She suddenly stopped reading and went as stiff as a board. Then she turned around and said to him, "Are you *the* Walt Disney?"'

When I was there, he took us on a tour of the original Disneyland, which was just being built. The Swiss Family Robinson tree was just going up. It was all steel, towering God knows how high, an immense thing. And he said proudly, 'And they say only *God* can make a tree!' That was the only time I ever glimpsed a major ego at work.

The next film I worked on was *A Funny Thing Happened on the Way to the Forum*. I had designed the stage version both in New York and London. United Artists had got Mel Frank to produce it and Dick Lester to direct it. They both had very different ideas about how they wanted to do the film; it was a battle royal between the two of them. I was in Spain building the set – acres and acres of the back-streets of Rome, twenty miles outside Madrid. It was at the most interesting stage – all lath and plaster and scaffolding; it looked like a Fellini fashion shoot. Mel Frank arrived and we drove out together and started walking around the set. He got redder and redder. Finally he blew his cigar out about fifty yards and said, 'What the f—— are you doing to me? This isn't ancient Rome! Ancient Rome's supposed to be wide open vistas, soaring marble, you've seen the Pearl and Dean advertise-ments!' I said, 'Dick wants to do the other side of it, the tacky, back-streets version.' 'You've got to change it!' he said. 'I can't change it,' I replied, 'you've got to talk to Dick.' He said, 'Dick? You've got to have a mind of your own, boy, and think *my* way!'

In the theatre, the designer establishes the visual funnel

through which the audience experiences the piece. It's almost as if you're selecting the frame for the shot. Whereas in movies you don't have any part in that, unless you happen to have done the storyboard. You're more or less making a manageable environment from which the director and cinematographer will select the images. You're crucial at the beginning, but once everybody's track shoes are on, it all goes out the window.

In a way it *is* childish, working in movies. You know when you're a child you have a passion, a craze, for playing with your train set. It's like that. But if you think, 'If we get this train set right it'll make a lot of money,' it's not the same thing at all.

Most film directors are very visual. It's the accounts department that thinks design is a necessary evil. On *The Boy Friend* we changed the notice on the art department building door to 'Background and Frocks', so it would be less offensive.

I make a point – to the fury of many people – of not doing two jobs in a row that have even the faintest visual connection with each other. So I move from *Anything Goes* to *Waiting for Godot*. I love starting from scratch. Doing costume drawings, I even try to come up with a different style of drawing, to keep myself interested – to find out what part of the visual alphabet this animal is. I like to use a different set of muscles each time.

On the *Orient Express*, since everybody in it was a star they were all in awe of each other. There was Richard Widmark looking at John Gielgud and thinking 'Holy shit!' And there was John Gielgud looking at Richard Widmark and saying 'Oh God, I'm such a fan of yours!' Everyone was fascinated by everyone else.

I also worked with Lumet on *Prince of the City*. He wanted it to start out like a regular street cop film, full of vitality. Then, as it moved into a story of conscience he wanted to try to strip everything away. He did this by the way he used the camera, from very fluid to more short, quick cuts. And as the film gets into the heads of the cops all the peripheral set dressing, and all the costume, bleeds away. In that film the palette went from rather garish to no colour at all. It was interesting trying to achieve this, because the film process fights against it, especially if it's something with dozens of sets, on location.

For instance, there was a scene in the kitchen, where we start to get inside the hero's head. So the normal process is that the prop man would say, 'Right, they're having coffee? We should have a milk carton here.' Suddenly things start to appear. Because of available funds, you're not allowed your special spy on the case, but I fixed it for one of my assistants to be there, as a touch-up artist. Nobody could figure out why this scenic artist kept saying, 'Get that red milk carton out of there!' When you see a film, all that attention to detail registers, subconsciously.

On the other hand, sometimes you have to exaggerate. You have to keep in mind not only what the camera sees but what proportion will get weeded out in the editing process, and compensate for that. For instance, there's a big wedding sequence in *Heartburn*, with huge floral displays. I had to do it way beyond what you'd see in real life, with masses more flowers, for enough to be left in the finished film. And the *Orient Express* train was not in any way real, it was an incredibly heightened version. The Lalique fixtures, the brass luggage racks, the dried flowers – we added more and more of them.

That was a movie meant to remind you of other movies, rather than real life. So when I was trying to find a Hollywood version of an Istanbul hotel that happened to be in England (because Albert Finney was also in a play in London at the time) I suddenly remembered, in the middle of the night, the Finsbury Park Astoria. The fountains, the balconies, those Moorish tiles . . . I remembered it because, when Julie Andrews was a teenager, she appeared at the Finsbury Park Empire on a music-hall bill, and I used to follow her round on the circuit. So we painted it up, and dressed it up with palm trees, and shot the scenes there.

Jonathan Lynn

Director, actor and writer: 'Clue', 'Nuns on the Run',
'Yes, Minister' (TV)

I started writing because I was out of work as an actor. In
1966 I rang my agent from Selfridges and said, 'John, do you
know where I am?' I hadn't heard from him for a long time.
He said, 'No, where are you, love?' 'I'm in Selfridges, selling
records. I've been doing it for three months.'

So I started writing. I had an idea for a TV play. When
you're starting, ideas seem to be like gold dust. But soon you
realize that ideas are the easy bit, it's executing them that's
the problem, because then you've got to do 120 pages.

I had this idea and I thought it would make a great TV
play. No – I didn't think it'd make a *great* TV play, that's
Hollywood talk. I thought it'd make a TV play. In Hollywood
'great' precedes everything, it's the minimum adjective. If you
say something's 'quite good' they think it's terrible.

For the next five years I carried on acting, and writing in
my spare time. I wrote a lot of situation comedy – fifty or sixty
episodes. Then I began to feel a certain contempt for the
audience – they weren't laughing at insights but at trigger
words like 'knickers'. Put 'knickers' into a line and they'd
laugh every time. So I became director of the Cambridge
Theatre Company for five years. During that time Tony Jay
and I started writing *Yes, Minister*, and finally I was writing
a sitcom I really cared about.

The first movie I ever wrote, way back in 1974, was called
The Internecine Project – awful title! I'd called it something
else. I went on to the set the first day and I was horrified to
see the star (James Coburn) and the director arguing about

which version of an important speech they should use – I hadn't written either version.

I asked if I could see a copy of the shooting script, and one of the assistants phoned the producer and said, 'There's someone here who says he wants a copy of the script.' So I went home.

I didn't do another film for ten years. Then I came over here to write *Clue* for John Landis. In the end he asked me to direct it instead. I would have written it differently if I'd known *I* was going to direct it. In the end, it only half worked. Truffaut said, about films, 'At ten in the morning, on the first day, you set out to make the perfect film. By ten past ten you've blown it.'

What one doesn't realize is that, unlike TV, a film that doesn't work follows you around forever, like a stray dog that you've kicked out of the house. People go on seeing it! That had never crossed my mind. It's made me a lot more cautious.

Having been an actor helps me as a director – I know that it requires courage to be an actor. The disadvantage is that I'm sometimes too sympathetic – it's harder to push people when you've done it yourself. If I have to get tough, I get too upset.

As a writer, it's wonderful working with somebody else. When you're writing by yourself it's no good coming up with an interesting possibility, either for a funny line or funny situation, unless you can see where it goes and how to restore it. With a partner, though, you can throw ideas into the air and he can come back with a funny response. It makes it much more fun, and much easier. When we were writing *Yes, Minister*, Tony and I never had a cross word.

The film industry here sees itself differently from the industry in Britain. Hollywood is about entertainment; the British film industry believes it's about art – or would like it to be. I think that underestimates the art that's required in creating good entertainment.

Humour is very different, too, between the two countries.

Even though we both speak the same language, it's quite hard to get it right on both sides of the Atlantic. The film I've just finished, *Nuns on the Run*, was previewed both here and in England and it got laughs at different places. Until you know enough about what people care about and worry about – mainly what they worry about – until then, you can't be funny about it. Comedy is about recognition. Billy Wilder didn't do comedies when he first came here, he did dramas like *Double Indemnity*.

I've written some American screenplays, but I have someone here who 'translates' my English into American. The idioms are different. For instance, I once made a reference to 'swings and roundabouts' and they didn't understand it. For a start, they call roundabouts 'carousels'; and then the idiom doesn't exist anyway. In this latest film, which is British, I've done my utmost to keep the English character of the writing and yet not use any phraseology that would mystify Americans.

In a funny way, I'm starting again, here.

Percy Adlon

Film director: 'Sugar Babies', 'Bagdad Cafe', 'Rosalie Goes Shopping'

Up until recently we made pictures for a very small art-house audience. Then we found this nice little Bagdad Cafe story, we picked it up, like a desert flower, watered it, and then everybody liked it, all around the world.

The little place in the desert, the Bagdad Cafe, it didn't exist. We went to this place, to the last gas stations before Las Vegas. The entire town was just gas stations, coffee shops and a railway terminus. I like the desert. For me it's the zero feeling, the feeling that anything is possible. You get the drama because there's nothing else there.

We looked at the map and there was a place called Bagdad. So I said, 'Let's go there.' But we didn't find it. So we asked somebody, and they said, 'Last month we pulled down the final remnants, and the wind blew and the sand covered it up.' So this was a nice chance for a writer to re-create a place that wasn't there any more.

So we made the film. Then, recently, I was at the Edinburgh Film Festival and a man came to me and said, 'I know the real Bagdad Cafe.' I said, 'What are you talking about?' He said, 'I have a photograph of it. I was a pilot in 1943 and I was on military reconnaissance. I'm sure that I photographed the Bagdad Cafe from above.' He sent me the photo. I got goose-pimples because it looked exactly as I had pictured it. It's strange, that you've invented something that existed.

I started as an actor. That's why the actors in my films feel comfortable that they are playing together nicely like instruments in an orchestra. What I'm doing is a musical thing;

I haven't much interest in political or didactic or psychological stuff. I like to leave some space in the story for improvisation. When I start, I just have a skeleton. Then I do a lot of homework. I learned this when I was making documentaries – I made over 150 documentaries for Bavarian TV. Making documentaries is improvisation and instinct. You're a hunter. You get the smell of the deer, you think this could be the place where it could come out in the evening. Then you tell your story on the editing table. It's based on what you've got and not necessarily what you wanted to get.

But feature film-making is what *I* want to get, and I have to do my homework. This means I have to find a style. I work with my cameraman for three weeks from nine to three every day, preparing shot by shot, angle by angle, colour by colour.

I'm looking for colours that fit the fiction – I don't copy the colours in real life. When you start filming, the camera just catches everything. So you have to be careful to eliminate the colours you don't like, and to emphasise colours you want to make important. This is my homework. Once this is done,

I was cast because I'm YELLOW - and now he's using a RED filter...

then I'm free for extraordinary things to happen because I'm not worried about the basic stuff. Even if I've had a bad night, or I'm in a bad mood, I still have the stuff from the preparation. We used warm golden and yellow colours in *Bagdad Cafe* because it's about friendship. This was the key to everything.

I have always been – together with my wife – writer, director, producer, editor. I don't know if I could direct another person's script, because I've never learned directing, I've only learned how to realize my own images. I write a short story and then we write together. I need somebody, like needing someone to supervise me when I'm doing my homework. And then, if I'm stuck in a certain part of the script, my wife says, 'Let's solve this problem later. Go on!' Then I go on, and maybe the problem isn't there any more.

Being a stranger here, in America, I have certain freedoms. I feel pretty comfortable working in English, though I don't know the language very well. The English language makes everything a lot easier. It's more relaxed, it's less formal, and it's shorter. I'm not very keen on a lot of dialogue. I think dialogue is one of the ingredients of the meal, but not the most important.

I write my scripts in German, but I'm listening in my head to the English translation. A dialogue in real German sounds terribly different from English, but because I know a little English I can imagine how it would sound – I'm writing my German *towards* how it would sound in English. Then I have a person in Munich, an American, and he translates my scripts into English.

But remember, for me language isn't the first priority. Film is about light and emotions. When I go to the movies I'm looking for certain feelings – emotions, body language, mood, music. I don't want too much explanation. It's like in dreams – you don't get too much explanation in dreams, do you?

I love it here in Los Angeles. It's just a big playground. It suits me, because film-making is a *childish* activity – but a childish activity that gets results!

Leah Adler

Steven Spielberg's mother

Every Saturday, so I wouldn't do them in, I used to dump my four kids in a movie theatre that showed non-stop kids' films. That's the only reason I'm halfway sane. Years later, Dick Cavett asked Steven, 'How come you know so much about these cliff-hanger films?' And he said, 'When I was a kid my mother used to dump me off. And that's what gave me my start.'

We bought Steve a movie camera as a Chanukah present. Once, we were leaving on vacation and we asked him to film us and the camper pulling out of the driveway. I got real annoyed at him because he was down on the ground, aiming the lens at the hub-cap. 'Steve!' I yelled. We have that footage and is it stunning! The wheels spinning, and then it pulls back . . . I guess he would have been about fourteen then.

Most of the time, my kids were in the backyard fighting. None of them went to college. Steve couldn't get into any university. We got him through high school – I wrote his term papers and typed them until three in the morning; then I'd run to school and lie to the teacher, saying he had flu. He was a lousy student but we all rallied round him. When time came for college he was totally unacceptable. He went to Long Beach State for one semester but that was it.

Then he did a little film called *Ambling* – a 20-minute art film, his room-mate put up the money for it – and it played as a filler in one of the theatres and the rest is history.

Was he bright? He didn't *act* bright. He wasn't a reader – he only read comic books. I very rarely walked into his room,

The in-flight movie
is anything you like –
So long as it's by Spielberg ...

except to get his dirty clothes, but now I know he was writing. The reality is, when you have four kids you go shopping for food and you cook the food and you take them off each other's throats. There's no perspective.

Where does it all come from? One of my uncles in Odessa was a lion-tamer. He was called Boris but he was billed as 'Leroy: The Youngest Lion Tamer in the World'. Another uncle was a Shakespearean actor in the Yiddish theatre. My father never entered a room just walking – it was a Nijinsky leap; he played a beautiful Russian classic guitar too, no lessons. And I'm a pianist.

I'm divorced from Steve's father, Arnold. He is very bright. He's a successful engineer. He thought Steve was a total loss because he flunked maths. But I think Steve's like me – he's got a grasshopper mind, he's bored easily. Maybe that's why he didn't do well at school. Now he's got a mind like a steel trap. He's educated himself.

It's wonderful – when I want to go anywhere I can sometimes take Steve's plane. All that cabinetry! When you close the door it goes ker-plunk. It seats about twenty people; there's beds, and a TV and a phone. They bring me kosher food. The funniest part is – you go to the airport, you get on it, they close the doors and you *go*! They don't wait for anybody. And yet Steve is still a regular meat and potatoes person.

Roddy McDowall

Actor: 'How Green Was My Valley', 'My Friend Flicka', 'Planet of the Apes', and many more

I was born in 1928 in England. My mother was mad about the movies; she was one of those creatures who were totally mesmerized by that new art form. She managed to put both her children – my sister and me – into the movies. I did some quick-quota films – with Will Hay, George Formby and others – I did about twenty-five. Then, when war broke out, we came to America and through a fluke, within two weeks, I'd landed the part in *How Green Was My Valley*. I was twelve then, and I was in movies for the next ten years.

That period was very exciting to me. I loved being in the movies. My schoolroom was at 20th Century Fox and MGM, where I worked. I didn't meet anyone outside the business. I didn't feel spoilt, though I know it was a very privileged life. Some of the studio kids didn't like it, but I liked it very much. I loved the movies and went three times a week. I was also tremendously interested in silent films, which were an anachronism by then. There was a movie theatre on Fairfax which showed silent films and I used to go there. I met a lot of those actors, and retained lifelong friendships with Pola Negri, Harold Lloyd, Buster Keaton . . . No one else paid much attention to them by then, but they were just riveting to me.

A studio pretends to be a big, benevolent, happy family but actually it was a rather cold, commercial business. Every case is individual, it doesn't matter if it's a child or an adult – it's as tumultuous for some people as it's rewarding for others. We all fantasize and glamorize the profession, which is part of its mystique. But most of the glamour, you know, is fabricated. It's really just a lot of people working very hard. In my childhood I thought I 'belonged' to this family, but I didn't because actually there was no such thing. That was hard to swallow because I wanted to belong.

Was I spoilt? Not really – in fact, one of the problems, in my early adult life, was that I was overdisciplined and overpolite. It was very hard for me to let it all out. This is because it's a very organized life. Everyone has to go through 'their rebellion' to find out who they are, but it's very hard if you're a child actor, or a child of enormous wealth, or great poverty. Then there are tremendous obligations; the pressure is enormous.

As a child I had talent but no craft. I had concentration; I had a fertile imagination and I cared enormously, so I could commit myself. There was no problem when I was working with wonderful actors and directors. But if I got into films that were less than that, I didn't know what to do. So I'd think of what had worked before. I was derivative, stealing from myself – not even stealing from anything I knew anything about! I was stealing from my own remembered instincts.

The fascinating thing was that when I began to investigate the craft of acting as a grown-up, when I went to New York, it took me months to realize what everyone was talking about. A lot of people remain brilliantly instinctive and talented and never have a lesson in their lives. I was one of those mechanisms that was enormously self-conscious in my adolescence. My mother couldn't understand it because, after all, I was a star. But I didn't know what I was doing, which was embarrassing.

When I was seventeen my agent said to me that I'd never work again. I felt 'That's rubbish! My life can't be over now.' So I went to New York. I was fortunate because it was a very productive time, it was the beginning of live TV. Otherwise, I don't know what would have happened to me. It only lasted for a decade, that live TV bonanza.

But I was still insecure – I still am! Acting is the only profession I know where the accumulation of your expertise and excellence counts for nothing. It's a very peculiar pro-fession. It's not like being a lawyer or dentist – you hang out your shingle and some fool's going to come in because you've got a DDS after your name. I still feel that the last job I've done is the last I'll ever get, that the phone may not ring again – and so many times it has been! The slings and arrows of so many careers!

Bette Davis – she had three or four careers. She once took an ad, saying 'I need a job'. Joan Crawford, she had terrible problems. It's fascinating when you know about it and you know the film that re-established their careers. With Gary Cooper it was *High Noon*, and Deitrich it was *Destry Rides Again*. And careers can be short-circuited by the most peculiar things over which actors have no control – it has nothing to

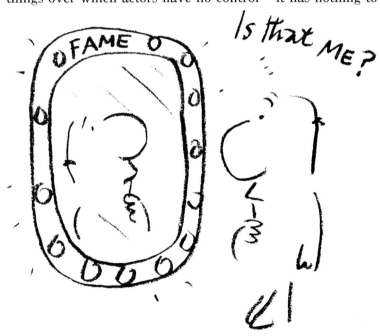

do with talent. What caused the demise of Gloria Swanson was the Depression. There was nothing wrong with her but the public couldn't accept, in the Depression, the opulence of her screen persona. That's why Shirley Temple, Will Rogers and Marie Dressler became operatic sort of successes – society needed and could deal with that sort of hope. At the end of the war, the reason Montgomery Clift became such a huge star was because the public was sick of all that macho stuff and they needed a new voice and spirit, something gentler.

And take a film like *It's a Wonderful Life*, in 1946 – it was a sensational disaster! It broke the company that made it; Jimmy Stewart thought he'd never work again. It was too schmaltzy. Society couldn't accept the Capra canon, because there had been a war. The Capra dream didn't have any hold on reality, at all. But *now* it has a hold – now it's revered! It's part of the American Dream.

It's always difficult, growing up, but it's more difficult if you're under a magnifying-glass. Even as an adult, when someone looks at you in the street it's normally because of some sexual persona you have. There's no other reason they would turn around. But if you've been famous, you never know for sure. Are they looking at 'you', or are they looking at *you*?

Carrie Fisher

Actress: 'Shampoo', 'Star Wars', 'When Harry Met Sally'
etc.; and author of 'Postcards from the Edge' (daughter
of Debbie Reynolds and Eddie Fisher)

When I was little I wanted to be Dorothy Parker. I figured
out very early on that she was half-Jewish – *I'm* half-Jewish;
she was 5' 1½" – *I'm* 5' 1½". She had dark eyes and dark hair.
Then later I realized: she was alcoholic – *I'm* alcoholic. She
was unsuccessful with relationships – *I'm* unsuccessful with
relationships! So that's what I wanted to be. And I made up
poems and puns – very seriously, all the time.

When I started acting, I stopped. I just fell into acting, I
was never interested in it. Then I'd only write when I was
upset. It was a way of distracting myself, and that's a kind of
hobby with me, distancing myself from myself. I feel that I
might as well write from experience because I've had such a
weird life. And instead of it using me, *I* might as well use *it*.
When I kept a journal, as a kid, I did it in this weird way, as
if it was going to be read. I had this strong sense of being
watched. But I was in a family that was being watched! So I
would act as if I was worthy of the watching.

My background is showbusiness and alcoholism. It's a need
for attention and an inability to cope. I have no coping skills.
The way that my family copes is work. Or staying up all night
drinking. I've never seen anyone in my family relax. It's all
to do with an obsession with product and *things*.

I think showbusiness draws people to it that have something
to prove. Their behaviour is compulsive. The kind of ambition
you need, it's pretty searing. You really have to focus on it.
Never mind just getting there – *staying* there, that's going to
make you real nervous.

HOW TO MEASURE
YOURSELF
AGAINST
DOROTHY PARKER.

Height

- FAME
- ALCOHOL
- NEUROTIC   5ft
- JEWISH

I grew up in the back end of celebrity. My parents had peaked when I was born. So it was downhill after that. I was becoming conscious as it was becoming less easy for them. They were still wealthy, but there were less parts available. So I grew up knowing that the best it could be – which is what *I* had – was very unstable.

I don't know my father so well. My mother had a nervous breakdown when I was a teenager. At forty she got a divorce, he went broke and she had to support him. And at forty, as a female in the movies, it's not happening so much for you. It was, like, panic the whole time I grew up.

So I learned to tell myself stories all the time, it was like a drug. The people that I know who are funny, it's because they have to tell themselves a better version of the truth. Or at least one with a punch line. My version of the truth was always: 'Oh no!' I learned to say 'Oh no!' in a thousand different ways, with a couple of accents and some one-liners if I could. The funniest people I know have not necessarily had the weirdest childhoods, but they've had the weirdest reaction to their childhoods.

When I was little I realized that people were going to envy me. But when you're a kid you just want to belong – every kid wants to belong, that's why they end up taking drugs, they want acceptance from their peers. But I realized I had this thing which could make me an object of envy, that could make me conceited or spoiled, so I ended up becoming an apology in advance. I'd tear it down before you could, I'd make fun of it. It's like walking in saying 'I'm fat!' before anyone else can.

My mother comes from Texas; I call it blue-blooded white trash. They both went from nothing to movie stardom. There's no preparation for that. They went from no money straight into the American Dream, which is supposed to be everything you want.

My father's not funny, but he's charming. My mother, she's funny. She's a roughie-toughie, a survivor. Unfortunately, if you're a survivor you keep getting shit to survive, to show off your gift, and I ended up inheriting that quality – I end up having shit to survive too.

I have her bravado and probably her speed, but the content is different because I didn't have to get where I am, I was *born* where I am. To stay there, it needs a different muscle. But she invented herself. She's a career woman. When I told her what I was getting for my second book – it was a considerable amount of money – she said, 'It's not enough!' I don't know if I'd have functioned so well if I'd had a mother who said, 'Whatever you do, it's OK with me, baby.' My mother's a great career model. But the other stuff? I think I fall between the cracks.

Most movie stars' kids are alcoholic or dead or incredibly fucked-up. I mean, do *you* want to be Dostoevsky's kid? You don't want to follow a great act, it's hard enough having an act anyway. I can sing, but I chose not to go into the same area of showbusiness as my family. No way am I going to try to compete, with the same skills as them. It's hard enough competing anyway. But in some way I'm always going to be compared with my parents. I'll never lose it – it's just part of the freight I carry.

I never thought I was attractive. I grew up with two adorable parents. My mother came home from the studios looking gorgeous, and I looked in the mirror and I looked like a thumb. I thought I must have been adopted. Here were these two glamorous people and I was this nebbishy accident. So I developed my humour as a way of justifying my position.

And these are people who are also cute for ever! There isn't a real precedent for maturing in my family. Nobody gets old, they just get face-lifts. In Hollywood you can't grow old with grace, you can't grow old at all.

But there *is* a precedent, in my family, for being the centre of attention. Imagine everybody being the centre of attention! It's like all bricks and no mortar. The building's going to fall.

I was a chorus girl at sixteen, in my mother's show, and then an actress from seventeen. I haven't got a literary background. I haven't had any formal education, I'm like this raw amorphous ball of unstructured mess. Hollywood isn't my fantasy, it's my reality. I liked the reality behind the fantasy, I liked crews. I liked hanging around the temporary 'family' of a movie. Doing *Postcards* and being on the set as the writer was a dream – my skin can break out, I can retain fluids and it doesn't matter. I can hang around with the crew and I don't have to be on the call sheet at five in the morning. Acting never really used up my whole personality; writing does.

Writing meetings are so much more interesting than acting meetings. I was always the best acting meeting you could have – you'd never give me the part, but you'd always remember what we talked about. I'm manic.

When I wrote *Postcards from the Edge* I sent it to Mike Nichols, because I'd known him since I was seventeen and I know what he likes. Since there's no structure to my book – I say proudly – I did two drafts, one adapting it from the novel form to screenplay form. Based on that, we did an outline. Then we had to decide what it was about – which was obsession. But you can't make a movie on a theme. So – I had one scene that had the mother in it, and from that we worked out a story about herself and her mother. And that's what it's about.

I learned fast with Mike. With him, it was like 'the secret handshake of shared sensibility'. I have no education but I have this experience now and I can re-write a scene until it works, because I could do that as an actor, I could re-do a scene until it worked. Making the movie was great. It was like an Agatha Christie movie, this boat full of great actors. I thought it would capsize. We came in two weeks under schedule – that's never heard of!

I was famous when I was twenty, in *Star Wars*. Well, Princess Leia was famous, and I was only famous because I happened to be wearing her clothes, not because I did it particularly well or anything. That, again, was *adjunct* celebrity. But this celebrity of being a writer has the most to do with me of anything. There's no way of *accidentally* being a writer.

I don't think of myself as a *real* writer. But I have some tricks I can do. I have a high verbal skill and a speed I can use. I look like a little kewpie doll from Hell, but I can turn a verbal trick. Nothing really reassures me, but this reassures me slightly.

Billy Wilder

*Writer and Director: 'Five Graves to Cairo', 'Double
Indemnity', 'The Lost Weekend', 'Sunset Boulevard',
'Ace in the Hole', 'Sabrina', 'The Seven Year Itch',
'The Spirit of St Louis', 'Love in the Afternoon',
'Witness for the Prosecution', 'Some Like It Hot', 'The
Apartment', 'Irma La Douce', 'The Fortune Cookie',
'The Private Life of Sherlock Holmes', 'The Front Page',
'Fedora' and others*

I'm sorry I can't talk to you, but I'm writing my own book.

Saul Bass

Title designer for: 'A Walk on the Wild Side', 'The Man
with the Golden Arm', 'Around the World in Eighty
Days', 'Psycho', 'Broadcast News', 'Big' and many
more. Also film director: 'Phase IV' and others

I started as a graphic designer, so I came into film after I'd
established myself. I came out to Hollywood in the early
fifties and hooked up with Otto Preminger, doing symbols for
advertising campaigns promoting his films. When I'd designed
the symbol for *The Man with the Golden Arm*, we thought,
Why not animate it and put it at the beginning of the film, in
the titles? For a long time I'd been feeling that the long roll of
names, titles and credits that came on while people chit-
chatted and made themselves comfortable in their seats was
being wasted – that this neutral moment could be utilized to
set the tone and the mood of the film. So I animated the arm
of the title – I made a series of abstract bars and branches –
and Elmer Bernstein wrote a jazz score. And in a sense I
reinvented the motion picture title. It had once been terribly
rich and innovative but had then become really quite dull.

So I began to do titles for various films, and I worked for
an extraordinary group of film-makers – William Wyler, Billy
Wilder, George Stevens, John Frankenheimer and, of course,
Hitch. Titles are really miniature films – you go through the
entire process: you conceive it, produce it, direct it, edit it,
work with the composer and so forth. So I got an incredible
course in film-making with the great directors.

At first I did mood-settings. Then I progressed to prologues
which dealt with the time before the film began. Finally I
found myself doing sequences within the film; directors would
ask me to do various things other than titles. They ranged
from the intimacy of the shower sequence in *Psycho* to the

race sequence in *Grand Prix*, where I was directing anything from three to eight cameras and working with twenty cars and 2,000 extras. I also did the battle scene in *Spartacus*.

Psycho was a rich experience. I'd worked for Hitch before, doing the titles for *North by Northwest* and *Vertigo*. When *Psycho* came up he asked me to work not only on the titles but on several sequences in the film too. One was the shower sequence, the other was where the detective gets killed on the stairs, and I also worked on the discovery of the mother's corpse. I worked on the house, too. Hitch wanted something that would make it look strange and foreboding. I looked at the notion of lighting it in some way but that was terribly hokey. Finally I evolved what was a very simple and curious device: I matted in some time-lapse cloud footage. However, it wasn't heavily time-lapsed – when you looked at it, the night clouds just moved a little faster than clouds normally move, even with wind. What you feel is that something weird is going on but you don't know why. It just feels wrong.

A rather wonderful thing happened to me on that film. I story-boarded the shower sequence and got Hitch's approval. But I wasn't sure it would work. I was nervous about it, so I grabbed one of the extras, rented an old clockwork camera, shot some stuff and just shwacked it together. It seemed quite do-able. When we got on the set Hitch was sitting in his tall director's chair in Buddha-mode – his hands folded over his belly – and he said to me, 'Why don't you set up the first shot?' So when I'd set it up I turned to Hitch and said, 'It's ready for you.' He turned to me and replied, 'Go ahead. You know what to do.'

So I swallowed, and gulped, and said, 'Er . . . camera roll!' And I shot the entire sequence. It was an amazing experience.

Frankly, I was amazed that Hitch accepted my point of view about *Psycho*. His point of view was always long, interesting and complicated shots. The shower sequence was a wholly different thing stylistically; it was staccato, it wasn't Hitchcockian in character.

Then I got tired of beginnings and middles; I decided I wanted to do something that had a beginning, a middle and an end. So I started making short films, working collaboratively with my wife Elaine, and I directed a science fiction picture called *Phase IV* for Paramount. But I've never been really hungry enough for the hassle of making full-length films. It's so very hard to get a feature off the ground. There are so many good directors who haven't made a film for four or five years. You can get the whole deal set up, then suddenly the studio people change, somebody breaks their commitment, the umbrella for the film moves and you're left standing in a downpour.

I love film in any manner, shape or form but I think titles are cute. It's a darling little piece of film to fool with.

I thought it was a bit of an anti-climax after the TITLES...

Vincent Price & Coral Browne

Actors

VINCENT PRICE: *'Laura'*, *'House of Wax'*, *'The Fly'*,
'Theatre of Blood' etc.
CORAL BROWNE: *'Auntie Mame'*, *'The Killing of Sister
George'*, *'An Englishman Abroad'* etc.

V.P.: I got into horror films by chance. I was in the first 3-D
picture *The House of Wax*; it became a huge success and a
cult film. That led to the others. They were great fun to do;
sometimes it was hard to keep a straight face – for instance,
when I was making *The Fly*, with Herbert Marshall. It's
impossible to keep a straight face when your nephew is a fly
with a human head.

They were really Gothic tales. They've never stopped playing – for which I get nothing, I hasten to add. Coral would
be bedecked with diamonds if I got residuals.

I also did a lot of light comedy. All the TV I did was
take-offs of my own stuff. It was great fun; I worked a lot
with Jack Benny and Red Skelton. So I never felt I was
trapped. Anyway, I didn't do all that many – I've made 110
pictures and only twenty of them were horror pictures. For
instance, I was in *Laura*, with Gene Tierney. I did five pictures
with her. She was extraordinary; she doesn't date . . .

C.B.: . . . I think that, in acting, she was before her time. She
had a wonderfully natural sort of acting – if you look at films
of that period the ladies weren't all that natural. She had it
before Grace Kelly – it went Gene Tierney, Grace Kelly, and
then it got lost . . .

V.P.: Ava Gardner had it. So many of those really glamorous
girls were so much better actresses than anyone gave them
credit for. Jane Russell, for instance – in *Gentlemen Prefer*

Blondes she was really wonderful, terribly funny. She was as good as Marilyn Monroe.

But if you did a picture with Jane Russell you did a picture with Howard Hughes at the same time. Nobody ever saw him, but he'd call the set every day; 'Hello, this is Howard!' he'd scream over the phone – he was as deaf as a post – 'What happened today? Tell me all about it!' I never met him.

C.B.: I came to live in Hollywood sixteen years ago, when I married Vincent. It's quite a small community really, and everybody knows everybody else. I've only been to two of those really big, grand Hollywood parties since I've lived here. At one of them, the host had turned his house into a thirties night club. He brought the designer from London, and the cook from Paris . . . two orchestras . . . you've no idea what it was like. It was all tented and gauzed. On the tables were these tall vases filled with white orchids. The food was to die about. And two ladies were brought out from London to do the calligraphy for the seating cards.

We went to this other one recently, given by Zsa Zsa Gabor for Barry Humphries. The trouble was, the invitation said to meet Dame Edna of London, but she forgot to introduce him to anybody. He didn't know anybody but us. She'd said 'Come to dinner' – and she'd invited three hundred people! The wine was unbelievable. I said at the bar, 'I'll have a glass of champagne.' And the waiter said, 'This *is* champagne – from West Germany.' It was maple syrup and old floor moppings and God knows what. Dinner was served at 11.15. It was absolutely superb – everyone had half a duck – but not around 11.15 at night. Then the cheesecake arrived; I hadn't got enough muscle-power to lift it. It must have come from West Germany too, from the concrete factory.

We just poked our noses into her sitting room. She had more pictures than we have, in this house – but they were all pictures of her. Every one of them.

Fiona Lewis

Freelance screenwriter

Writers are still at the low end of the scale in Hollywood. Basically everyone thinks they can write; if they had the time. The non-creative people are always jealous because they wish they could do it. They always think creative people are hysterical and want too much money.

When you hand in a script they say, 'That's nice,' and then you get four or five executives – about twenty, just out of Yale – saying 'I think we should change the ending;' all these clichés like, 'Act Three doesn't work for me', you know, or, 'Where's the *arc* of the character?' All that kinda stuff. If they like it they'll try and attach a director, but if two or three say no they're on to the next; they're bored.

There's the terrible pitch meeting where you have to go in and sell yourself like a stand-up comedian. They sit there and stare at you with no expression whatsoever. The best way, if you can afford it, is to write an original because then you don't have all this input from the studio. It's yours. You don't have this committee of people telling you what your characters should be like.

Talent is undefined in the movie business, so anyone can hustle their way in. Nobody really knows what makes a great movie. It's all about hanging in there. Hanging on and driving people insane. If you stick around long enough you do get something made. You always think, 'This is going to be the big one.' It's a bit like falling in love I suppose.

Polishing is the job every writer wants. Someone else has done all the hard work and all you have to do is dust off the

dialogue. Stars often come in and re-write the script. The classic story in Hollywood is the serious writer who comes in with a story about a love affair or whatever. By the time he's finished it's about a dog, a pony and two sex fiends. They always say they're going for the class, but in the end it's the commercial stuff.

You're always meeting the guy who pumps gas who has a script in his pocket to show you. I went to an eye doctor and he had a script about . . . an eye doctor. You always try and back out politely because then you have to read it and make comments on it. Before you know where you are you're having a script meeting with your eye doctor.

This is suburbia. It's not like London or New York, so when I go to a meeting in the studio I dress like a dyke or something. I wouldn't dream of going in there in a skirt.

You have to be serious in meetings. No jokes. You can't be flippant or ironic. The trouble is, they're all insecure and suburban. They're terrified of doing anything.

It's all about meetings and lunches and parking spaces really. The big thing for an executive is, how near is your parking space to the main building? That's the most important thing for them.

It's a hard job though. You have to be there at 7 a.m. You get home at 9 p.m. and have to read six scripts. You have no social life. The business is their big adrenalin rush. That's their sex.

A Hollywood producer once said, 'When I was in Florence doing an art course my teacher took me to the quarry and said, "Michelangelo could look at a stone and see the Pietá." And I said, "You know, that's how I feel. I look at a book and I see the movie."'

S. J. Perelman

*Author and screenwriter: 'Monkey Business', 'Horse
Feathers', 'Around the World in Eighty Days' etc.
(Interviewed by the author in 1978)*

I went out to Hollywood first in December 1930, soon after
Groucho hired Will Johnstone and me to work on *Monkey
Business*. It all began when I went to a performance of *Animal
Crackers* on Broadway – and I was so entranced that I went
to see the brothers after the show. Groucho explained to me
that they were interested in doing some radio. Johnstone was
then a working cartoonist and I myself had worked for five
years writing and drawing for *Judge* and the old *Life* magazine. We were both essentially comic artists. Johnstone had
worked for them before, on a vaudeville sketch.

Johnstone and I got into a huddle in a room for three days
and the only idea that we came up with was the notion of the
four Marxes as stowaways on a transatlantic liner – each one
in his own barrel.

Having thought of this, our inspiration completely gave
out. On the third day, the Marx Brothers rang up and asked
us to lunch. We put forth this idea, and to our complete
stupefaction Groucho turned to Chico and said, 'This isn't a
radio sketch, boys, this is our next picture.'

Before we had recovered our breath they took us by the
hand and led us to the Paramount building and introduced us
to Jesse Lasky. We were both signed to six-week contracts at
500 dollars a week. For us this was big money – especially
because the Depression had just started.

The Marx Brothers departed for Europe to appear at the
London Palladium and we started work on the screenplay.
Our supervisor was a man called Herman Mankiewicz. He

was a Teutonic, overbearing broth of a man who was famous for his cutting wit. He was also a great card-player and drunkard.

An interesting thing about the word 'supervisor'. The men who dominated movies then had all been either pack-peddlers or junk-dealers – like Mayer, Zukor. Sam Goldwyn, for instance, had been a glove-maker. The term 'supervisor' was a factory term.

Johnstone and I sat down and wrote what we thought was a screenplay. Neither one of us was experienced in this form – but we had picked up a lot of very professional terms: dollies, a trucking shot, iris down, etc., and we thought it necessary to cram all this nonsense into the script. We thought, in our innocence, that all these instructions would act as a guide to the director. We wrote about 125 pages in this fashion.

We were then summoned to read the script to the Marx Brothers. There were the three married Marxes with their wives. They had also picked up some dogs – huge creatures. There was also their dentist, their lawyers, their accountants. There were twenty-nine people and three dogs in that room. I began to read the script and I read all the instructions as well as the dialogue. When I got through there was a considerable silence. Chico turned to Groucho and said, 'Well, what do you think?' Groucho said audibly, 'Stinks.' Everybody rose and slowly left the room.

I said to my wife, 'Start packing.' The next morning the phone rang and Mankiewicz said, 'Come over and let's get to work.' It took us about six months to write a new script and that became *Monkey Business*.

Groucho considered me too literary. He often hurled this charge at me. In that picture, Groucho and Thelma Todd were making love and I had written the scene so that suddenly Groucho was to jump up and say, 'Come, Kappelmeister, let the violas throb, my regiment leaves at dawn.' And then he was to go into a parody of the famous scene from *The Merry Widow*.

Groucho read this scene and said, 'The trouble is that the barber in Peru won't get it.' He meant Peru, Indiana. I disagreed violently with him, because I think that Groucho was a master of parody. What happened eventually was that this whole scene was cut out, but that one line is still in the picture. It always gives me a thrill to hear that line.

Eighteen months later they hired me to work on *Horse Feathers* – in collaboration with Kalmar and Ruby. But the Marxes were boorish – Harpo was the nicest.

I went back to Hollywood whenever we were broke. This was the Depression. Hollywood could absorb writers; there were five big studios. The studios owned the cinemas and the bill was changed twice a week, so that an enormous amount of product was needed. There were over a hundred writers on the lot at Metro. All of us were on an assembly line – rewriting each other's pictures.

After the first novelty, it quickly became very boring. What films were about then – and what I think they are still about – was the unexpected. Those people prospered who had a quick mind and the ability to arrange shallow, trivial situations that were unexpected. It is a medium in which a lot of shallow people became successful. And the rewards were fantastic.

There were, however, some very charming and amusing people there. People whom I came to know and love, in fact. But actually, it was the most boring life I have ever experienced. The social life consisted of interminable dinner parties, where nothing was talked about but film, grosses, performances. It was like an industrial town where nothing but shoes are made . . . and where nothing but shoes were talked about.

And then the fact that the grass was always green, that the climate never changed. In the end it became so boring that you were almost out of your head to get away.

I worked on several pictures, usually on dialogue. It was felt that I had a penchant for dialogue rather than situations.

We were hired by Thalberg to work on this wretched thing called *Greenwich Village*, which was an almost indescribable pot-pourri of nonsense. Later on we were hired by Hunt Stromberg to work on *Sweethearts*.

There is always a courtship period between the producer and the writer, in which the producer asks the writer what he wants to work on. This is as formalized a ritual as a bullfight. If the writer is naïve at all – and he usually is – he comes up with a suggestion. So we suggested a play. Stromberg countered by asking us if we had ever heard of *Arms and the Man*. Stromberg wanted to combine *Arms and the Man* with *The Chocolate Soldier*. Then he said, 'Speaking of Victor Herbert, have you ever heard of *Sweethearts*?' At this our eyes capsized in our heads, because some of the sickliest music that has ever been written is that stuff. He then played some of this dreadful hogwash. 'That's what we are going to make,' . . . as though the idea had just appeared, like a Mazda bulb over his head. Well, we needed the work. We needed the money. So we numbly acceded. We figured that we could dress it up. You always think – well . . . things are bad but you gotta eat. We stuffed a psychiatrist into it . . . all kinds of things. My wife was then heavily pregnant with our first child, so we finally told Stromberg that she couldn't continue working on the picture. She retired from the scene and he hired Dorothy Parker and her husband, Alan Campbell.

Stromberg became intensely creative. He used to walk up and down, dictating voluminous notes about the characters, with two secretaries in the room and Dorothy Parker knitting a long shapeless garment that eventually became about 14 feet long and two feet wide. It looked like a stair carpet.

She had Winston Churchill glasses perched on the end of her nose and a look of . . . she was off in some other country. Every so often Stromberg would stop and say, 'Dorothy, what do you think of it so far?' And she'd look up over the top of her glasses and say, 'Oh, I do think it's marvellous, don't you?'

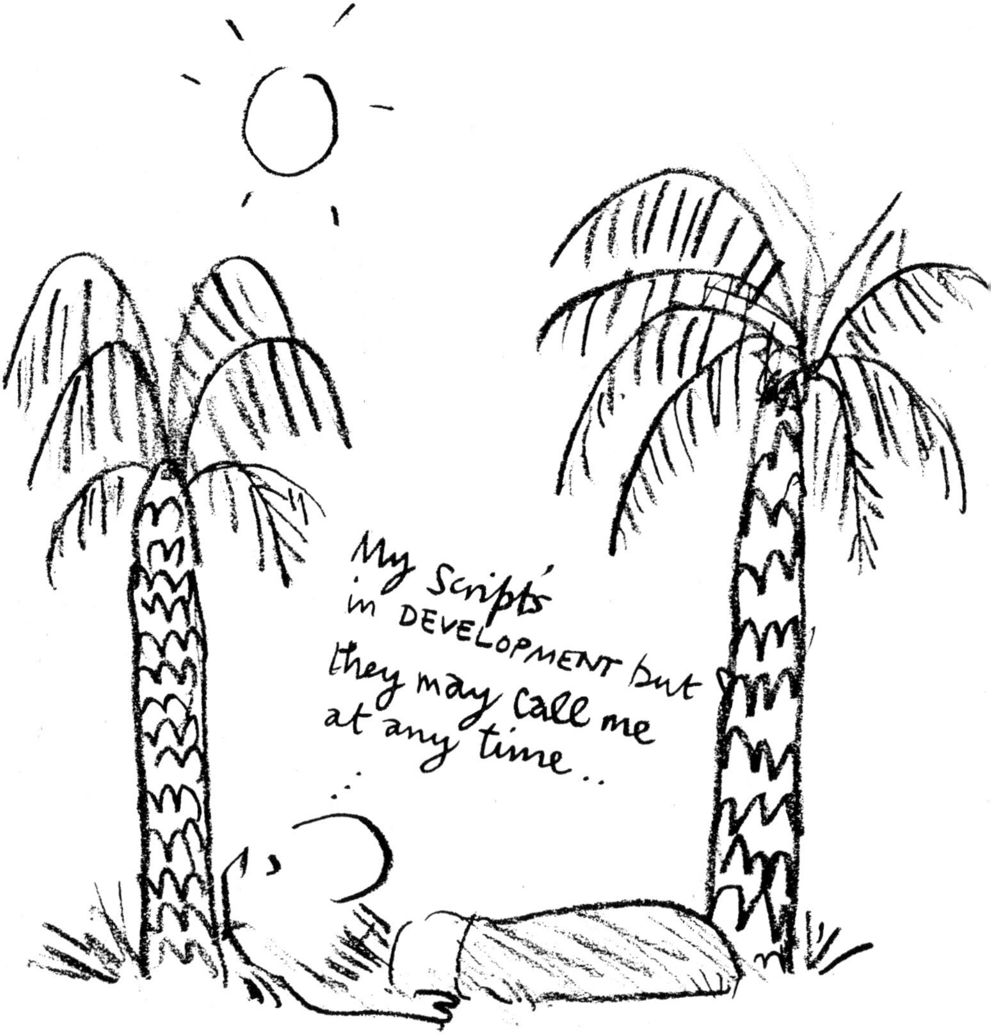
My Script's in DEVELOPMENT but they may call me at any time...

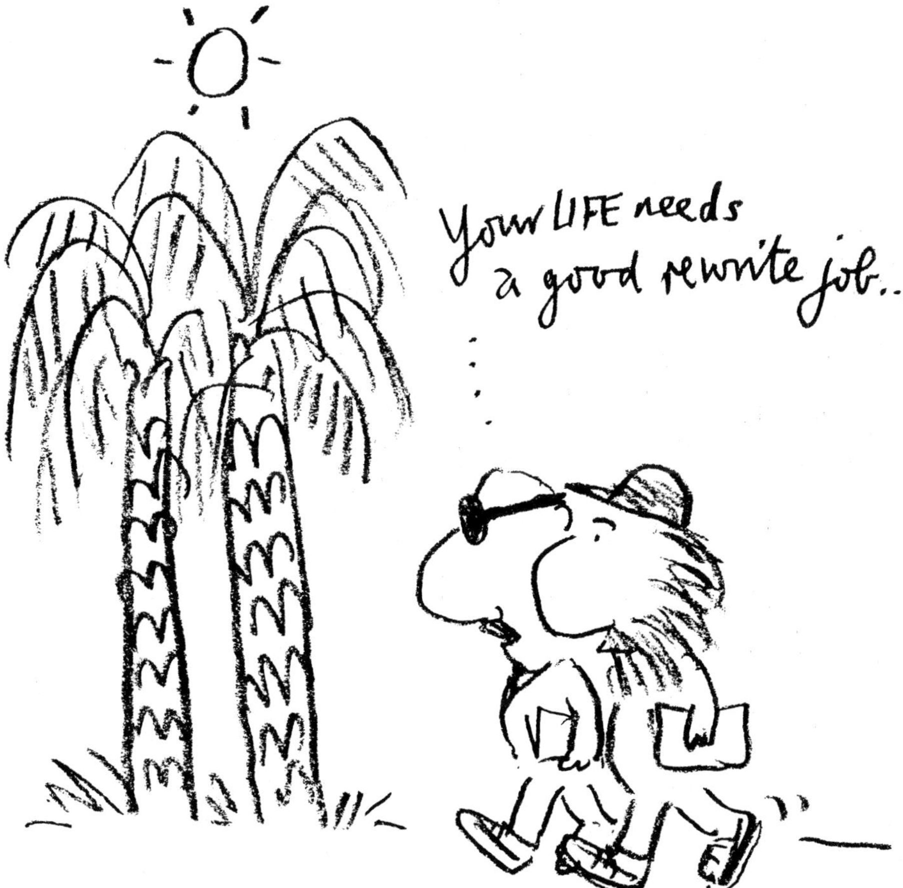
Your LIFE needs
a good rewrite job...

WARNING!
THIS AREA
CONTAINS CONCEPTS
and ATTITUDES KNOWN
TO CAUSE
HIGH BLOOD PRESSURE,
STRESS and
PARANOIA...
HOLLYWOOD